THERE'S A PRAYER FOR THAT...

D0584506

NORTHWESTERN PUBLISHING HOUSE
Milwaukee, Wisconsin

Cover Illustrations: Shutterstock
Art Director: Karen Knutson
Designer: Paula Clemons

Northwestern Publishing House
1250 N. 113th St., Milwaukee, WI 53226-3284
www.nph.net
© 2017 Northwestern Publishing House
Published 2017
Printed in the United States of America
ISBN 978-0-8100-2893-7
ISBN 978-0-8100-2894-4 (e-book)

23 24 25 26 27   12 11 10 9 8

Thank you to the following pastors for contributing prayers:
Dan Babinec, Jon Balge, Mark Barenz, Joshua Becker, Thomas Behnke,
Jeff Berg, David Bitter, Jeff Duquaine, David Endorf, Nathan Ericson,
Rob Guenther, Mark Hannemann, Andrew Hussman, Michael
Kampman, Mike Plagenz, John Raasch, Roger Riedel, Frank Rose, Jeff
Samelson, Gregory Sluke, James Sonnemann, Paul Stratman, Rolfe
Westendorf, Tim Westendorf, and Jay Zahn.

Contents

Prayers for the Church Year

1. Advent

Dear Father, the time is near for us to commemorate the birth of your Son, our Savior. We wish to receive him into our hearts. But heavenly Father, my heart is stained with sin. It is not fit as a home for one so pure and holy. There is pride, doubt, insincerity, false humility, and fleshly desire to want my will and not yours to be done. That is why I come to you and ask that you not only forgive me for this uninviting heart, but that you use your Word to root out all that makes me unfit to be called your own. Let me look forward, not only to the arrival of the Babe of Bethlehem but also the arrival of the King of kings as he comes in glory. Amen.

2. Christmas Eve

Thank you, Lord Jesus, for making this holy night so beautiful. The sparkling light, the joyful carols, and the beaming faces of family and friends cheer my heart every year. With the angels I glorify you; with the shepherds I kneel and adore you. With Mary I treasure up the wonders of your birth, and all year long I will ponder such unfathomable love that made you, both the Son of God and a human child, my Savior. Amen.

3. Christmas Day

Dear God of all glory, through eyewitnesses you have revealed to us your Son as the Babe of Bethlehem, as the Savior at the cross, and as the King of heaven. Help us, therefore, to praise him properly on his birthday, to receive him humbly in his grace, and to look for him to come again in glory, for his name's sake. Amen.

4. Christmas Table Prayer

Lord Jesus Christ, you were born as a human baby in great poverty. Yet hidden behind your humble appearance was the Lord of the universe. Open our eyes today to see precious signs of your love and mercy behind the joy of celebration, the faces of our loved ones, and the food that we now receive with thanksgiving. Amen.

5. Epiphany

Lord of glory, as the light of your star once led the wise men to Jesus, so the light of your Word has led us to see Jesus. Let your Word so shine in our hearts by your Spirit that each day we see Christ at the center of all we do. With him let us find comfort from sorrows, forgiveness from sins, and rest from turmoil. In his name, cause us to do good to others, to reveal him to the lost, and to praise your holy name. Amen.

6. Transfiguration

Dear Savior, how lowly you appear as you ascend the Mount of Transfiguration. As you go up with Peter, James, and John, you seem to be nothing more than an average human being. But, together with your disciples, today I see more than I expect. I see your face shining like the sun and your clothes "white as the light" (Matthew 17:2). You are the glorious Son of God. As I see you talking about your impending death in Jerusalem, I find comfort in knowing that God has come to earth and become a man in order to save me. Amen.

7. Ash Wednesday

Almighty God, as I begin this period of time set aside for reflection and repentance, help me to clearly see and be totally aware of my sinfulness. Convicted of my sins, lead me to a complete dependence on your grace and mercy in Christ. Help me change my sinful life, so that I may be an effective witness to your power at work. I come before you in Jesus' name. Amen.

8. Lent

Lord, I approach this season with mixed feelings. First, I feel terrible that I have sinned so severely to cause you such pain and suffering. I see your tortured body and think of the sins my hands have committed, the sinful thoughts I have had, the sinful words I have said, and the sinful things my eyes have beheld. For all my sins I am very sorry. Second, I feel good to know that you would take all my sins on yourself and give your life as a payment for them. For your forgiveness and my salvation, I am very happy. Should you wish for me to follow you in suffering, let me have the strength to bear it bravely, knowing that in the end I will have everlasting glory because you suffered and died for me. Amen.

9. Palm Sunday

O King most glorious, Savior most humble, hosanna to the Son of David, hosanna in the highest! Praise be to your name! Just as you rode into Jerusalem to fulfill God's promise for our salvation, so come into our lives to keep us on the way of salvation. You didn't waver on your way to the cross; forgive us when we waver on our way. Because your will is one with the Father's, so make our will one with yours. Glory be to God! Amen.

10. Maundy Thursday

Dear Savior, who came not to be served but to serve, you washed your disciples' feet as a parting token of your attitude of willing humiliation. Before you performed the ultimate act of self-giving by offering your life as a ransom for many, you also gave them and us a lasting testament of your loving sacrifice in Holy Communion. Teach me to treasure this blessed Sacrament and your holy example. Move me to serve others as you served. Amen.

11. Good Friday

Lamb of God, what a truly dark and empty day this would be for me if you had not willingly died on the cross! Your suffering and your death should have been mine. Impress upon me the joy this day should bring into my life. For by your death you made it possible for me to experience God's love and forgiveness every day. Help me never to live as though your death was for nothing. Rather, enable me to live as one who has died to sin and been made alive for righteousness. Hear me for the sake of your innocent suffering and death. Amen.

12. Easter

Living Lord and risen Savior, accept my alleluias and increase
my joy that comes from knowing that you have risen from
the dead. Comfort me with the assurance that my sins are
forgiven and eternal life in heaven is sure. Let the joy of the
Easter message lead me to go and tell the good news of your
resurrection to the people who don't know the true meaning of
Easter. Let the light of my faith in you shine brightly as I face
each day in the future and the day of my death on earth. I ask
this in your name, who rose for me. Amen.

13. Ascension

Lord Jesus, the thought of your glorious ascension into heaven
fills my heart with solace and comfort. Even though you
returned to heaven as the God-man, you are still my human
brother. And so you still empathize deeply with my every
infirmity. At the Father's right hand you whisper to him my
inmost needs, translating my sin-stained prayers and praises into
words of beauty for our Father's ear. Having you, my beloved
Brother, in heaven fills me with longing to join you in the
Father's house. Now I have proof positive that your offering
for my sins is acceptable to the Father. Glorious ascended
Savior, thank you for my salvation. Amen.

14. Pentecost

Holy Spirit, Comforter sent from Jesus, work in us by the Word
so that we may know the truth in Christ. Guard and keep us
in the faith that saves. Fill us with your power so that we will
delight in doing good works to the glory of God the Father.
And move us to be active in spreading the good news of Jesus
to people everywhere so that you may work saving faith in
their hearts also. In Jesus' name we pray. Amen.

15. Trinity

O Triune God, your threefold name was placed upon me when
I was baptized in the name of the Father and of the Son and of
the Holy Spirit. And this day I worship you, three divine persons

in one God. Grant me the grace to continue in this faith until I join the hosts of heaven that cry, "Holy, holy, holy," before your heavenly throne. Amen.

16. End of the Church Year

God of glory, eternal King, help us, we pray, to recognize the signs of the end times around us and to live each day with the realization that it could be the Last Day. Move us to hate what is evil and to cling to what is good. Keep us zealous in your service, joyful in hope, patient in affliction, and faithful in prayer, so that when the day comes, we will be among those looking up to see our Savior coming in the clouds. In his name we pray. Amen.

Prayers for Other Special Days

17. Reformation

As we gratefully remember the many blessings you have
showered upon your church through Dr. Martin Luther, we
know that he would protest if he were given any of the glory
that belongs to you, O God. As you began a great reformation
of your church by revealing to your chosen servant that your
righteousness is your gift to us through faith in Christ, so
create clean hearts in us, O God. Restore to us the joy of your
salvation so that we may boldly proclaim you to be our mighty
fortress. Amen.

18. Anniversary of the Presentation of the Augsburg Confession (June 25, 1530)

Lord Jesus, you charged your disciples with teaching everything
you commanded them, and then you promised that you would
be with your church to the end of the age. We give thanks for
those who confessed your teachings at the Diet of Augsburg
and for Christians of every time and place who face persecution,
danger, and even death for the sake of your truth. Continue
to bless your Word and those who confess and teach it so that
your gospel may spread to every tribe and language and people
and nation, and so that people now and in coming generations
learn your truth and find eternal life in you. Amen.

19. New Year's Eve

Eternal God, you are always the same and your years have no
end. In your mercy we close another calendar year. It has been
filled with your goodness to us. For this we humbly thank you.
It has known our sins, disobedience, and failures. For these we
ask your forgiveness and pardon in the name of Jesus Christ,
your Son and our Savior. Amen.

20. New Year's Day

Lord, at the beginning of this year we need you. Our days are
written in your book and only you know if I shall live through

this year that has just begun. Be merciful to me and forgive me all my sins. Bless my body and soul, my property, and my honor. Renew in me the knowledge of the promise you made to me at my baptism, so that I may have childlike assurance throughout this year that you will never forget me. Allow me, to the best of my ability, to live a year of service to you. Let this year be one which draws me closer to you as I serve my Savior Jesus. Amen.

21. Mother's Day

Dear Lord, I thank you for the gift of life you granted me through my mother. I also thank you for the time and love she has given me during my life. Bless mothers everywhere with love, patience, understanding, and strength to carry out their special work. Lead children everywhere to be thankful for their mothers. Keep families everywhere faithful to your Word. I pray this for Jesus' sake. Amen.

22. Father's Day

Gracious God, our Father, grant people everywhere the blessing of a loving father at home. In homes where fathers have neglected their duties or have been absent, help the children to persevere and to set their ideal for parenthood in your Word. Lord, thank you for my father. Direct me to honor, love, and respect him every day in every way. Keep all my family in the true faith in Jesus so that we may spend eternity together in heaven, for Jesus' sake. Amen.

23. Memorial Day

On this day set aside to honor those who have died in the service of our great country, O God, we thank you for giving us such patriotic citizens and a country that chooses to remember them. Also today we thank you for the saints who have gone before us in your service and have preserved for us the rich heritage of your gospel. We remember the blessings you gave to them and to us through them. Praise to you, O Savior, in your eternal glory. Amen.

24. Graduation

Look down with favor on all those who begin a new stage in their lives this day, dear Savior. Teach them to know you as the true wisdom of God, which has come down from heaven. Lead them to find fulfillment in their daily walks with you rather than in worldly success. And continually increase in them the understanding that, since we are pilgrims and strangers on this earth, the attainments of this life are not an end in themselves but a means of preparing for the commencement of the life to come. Amen.

25. Independence Day

As the United States pauses to commemorate its anniversary, we think of the many blessings you have made a reality for us, sovereign Lord. Forgive us our many complaints and our negligence in asking your blessings upon our land. Continue to allow us peace and bless all honest endeavors. Do not let our wonderful freedoms be abused or removed. Let justice and right prevail. Place loyalty in the hearts of our citizenry so that all may take an active role to do away with wrong and foster what is right. Above all, preserve our freedom to call upon you and to praise you. Bless our land! Amen.

26. Labor Day

Gracious heavenly Father, as our country pauses to contemplate the freedom to work and the employment opportunities that are available to us, may we never lose sight of the fact that it is only because of your grace and favor that we are able to work. Thank you, Lord, for the blessings of employment and work that I have had in the past and at present. May all that I do at work give glory to you and your precious name. I pray in the name of Jesus Christ, whom I love and serve. Amen.

27. Election Day

Thank you, God our Savior, for placing us in this country with the privilege to vote in free elections. Move many to exercise that privilege responsibly this day, and so guide the process to give us wise and effective rulers. Keep us mindful that, whatever the outcome, you are in control and, whatever the issues, the only lasting one is the issue of eternal life for all who love you in Christ. Bless us for his sake. Amen.

28. Veterans Day

Heavenly Father, we thank you for the selfless service of those who risked their lives to protect our nation, preserve our freedoms, and restore peace in the face of brutal aggressors. Grant relief to those who continue to experience emotional or physical agony from their days of combat. Give us a sense of responsibility for their welfare. Comfort those who mourn for loved ones who died while performing their duty to our country. Enlist all who are in our military forces into your church militant, that they may pledge eternal loyalty to Christ, our King, and know his peace. Amen.

29. Thanksgiving Day

Merciful God, you have done great things for us, and we owe you endless gratitude and love. We thank you, Lord, for each moment we enjoy in your blessed care, for each act of healing, for each meal to satisfy our hunger, for each friend and companion, for each little thing that keeps us going day by day. We especially thank you for the gift of your Son, Jesus. Accept our thanksgiving and prayers, O God. Pardon our sins. Help us overcome our weaknesses. And receive us at last into eternal glory, for Jesus' sake. Amen.

30. Thanksgiving Table Prayer

Lord God, our Maker and preserver, our hearts overflow with gratitude for the blessings you have showered upon us in the past year. Your mercies are new every morning; great is your faithfulness. Give us sincere appreciation for the freedoms we enjoy and for the wealth of our nation's resources. Whether we have much or little, make us generous to share what we have with those who have less. Enable us to use all your gifts as faithful stewards, avoiding carelessness and waste. Bless the food we are about to receive so that it may strengthen us in service to you and all people. In Jesus' name we pray. Amen.

Prayers for Occasions and Seasons of Life

31. Anniversary of Baptism

Dear Lord, I thank you for giving us your blessings of forgiveness of sins and eternal life through the Sacrament of Baptism. As I celebrate the anniversary of my baptism, I praise you for your grace toward me. Please continue to keep me in your grace so that your name is praised by my thoughts, words, and actions. I am forever grateful to live a renewed life in faith all to your honor, my Lord: Father, Son, and Holy Spirit. Amen.

32. Before Worship

Heavenly Father, I have come to worship you. Draw near to me in your gracious Word, and assure me of your loving-kindness. Curb my wandering thoughts so that with undivided attention, I may hear your voice and sing your praise. Amen.

33. After Worship

Grant, O Lord, that the lips which here have sung your praise may continue to glorify you in the world; that the ears which have heard you speak may be open always to your Word and closed to hatred and discord; that the tongues which have confessed your name may always speak the truth without fear; and that all of us who have worshiped together today may be united in true love for each other as you have loved us in Jesus. Amen.

34. Before Communion

Lord, I am not worthy to be a guest at your holy table. But you are the friend of sinners, and you will not cast me out. This bread is your body, which bore my sins upon the tree. This wine is your blood, which purifies me from all guilt. At your invitation, I come rejoicing. Receive me, my Savior. Amen.

35. After Communion

Thank you, Lord Jesus Christ, for nourishing me in this sacrament with your body and blood. You have given me forgiveness, life, and salvation. Let me always remain in you as a branch remains in the vine. Send me out in the power of your Spirit to live and work to your praise and glory. Amen.

36. Birthday

O God, our times are in your hands. Look with favor, I pray, on your servant as I begin another year. Grant that I may grow in wisdom and grace, and strengthen my trust in your goodness all the days of my life, through Jesus Christ our Lord. Amen.

37. Summer

Lord of wind and wave, guide us this summer in all that we do. Watch over us in our activities. Guard our lips against speaking evil, and let them glorify your name. Keep us mindful of our responsibilities as your representatives in this world. Cause us to be content with the earthly blessings you have been pleased to give us. Grant us peace, health, good weather, and faithful friends, according to your will. Deliver us from every evil, and preserve us unto your heavenly kingdom for Jesus' sake. Amen.

38. Before Vacation

We are waiting restlessly, Father in heaven, for the release from daily routine and the enjoyment of our vacation. Let our vacation days not be wasted or hurtful, but direct our activities in pleasant and renewing paths. May our vitality be rebuilt and our spirit renewed. Bring us back better equipped to serve you in our corner of your kingdom. Amen.

39. Vacation Time

Dear Lord Jesus, we are grateful for the opportunity to view the wonders of your creation. In our moments of rest, give us the inclination to reflect on your great wisdom, power, and love. Let us show, by our faithful use of your blessings, that gratitude which is proper in your people. Lead us to realize that all things depend on you and exist only according to your will. Protect us on our journey and bring us safely home. We commend ourselves into your gracious care. Amen.

40. After Vacation

Dear Lord, we are thankful that you have brought us home safely from our days of recreation. You have been with us to guard and protect us from evil and harm and to help us renew our energy. May the memories of these pleasant days whet our appetites for that promised great and unending rest in heaven with all its joys. Meanwhile, help us to fulfill our duties here joyfully in the strength you will give. Amen.

41. Safe Travel

Lord, let your holy and powerful angels attend us wherever we go, to keep us safe from all harm. We count on you for all our protection. Be with us to bless all of our travels and vacations. Keep us in mind of our salvation so that we serve you faithfully whether we are at home or far away. Amen.

42. When Away From Home

Lord Jesus, you once left your home in heaven and came to this world to live. Even here you had no fixed earthly home as you went about preaching and doing good. You know the feelings of those who are far from their homes. And so I ask for your blessing while I am away from home. Help me overcome the problems that I must face in a strange environment. Protect me so that no harm may come to me in body or soul. Guard my faith in you and bring me safely home again so that my loved ones and I may worship together and enjoy one another's company under your gracious blessing. In your name, dear Savior, I pray. Amen.

43. In School

Creator-Lord, thank you for the chance you have given me to learn about all that you have made and done and to grow in wisdom and knowledge. Bless my studies. When the material I am trying to master or the workload of my assignments becomes too much for me, give me courage to ask for help and the strength to persevere in the work. When classes seem boring and homework becomes tedious, help me to see how you are using my classes to prepare me for a life of service to you. Amen.

44. Learning to Drive

Heavenly Father, you have promised to watch over my coming and going on this earth. May I be alert and courteous, both for my own safety as well as the safety of other drivers. Keep me from impatience and do not let me become distracted so that no one may be harmed by careless or impulsive driving on my part. Bring me safely to my every destination, for the sake of Christ my Savior. Amen.

45. Looking for a Job

Loving Father, I praise you for the physical and mental abilities you graciously have given me and for my time on this earth to use them. As I search for a job, help me find a place and position where I can use my gifts to your glory, bring benefits to others, and gain the means to support my loved ones with the necessities of life. Don't let me become discouraged or anxious. Help me trust that you will lead me on the very best path so I can do all things faithfully and cheerfully out of gratitude to my Savior. Amen.

46. Moving Away

Dear Creator, I know that even before there was sin in the world, sinless Adam talked about people growing up and leaving the home of their youth (Genesis 2:24). But leaving a long-loved home must feel so different now from the way you first intended it—now that fear and tragedy have come into our lives. Calm my fears. Protect those I leave behind. If it is your will, let me see those loved ones again soon. Bless my new home. Help me make good friends there and to show them the love of your Son, in whose name I pray. Amen.

47. Entering Military Service

Almighty God, Lord of the nations and protector of all who put their trust in you, hear my prayer as I enter the military service of my country. Take me into your fatherly care. Help me find companions who will stand with me against those who reject and despise our Savior Jesus Christ. Give me strength to withstand the temptations with which Satan will attack me; and if in weakness I should fall, lead me to repentance and lift me up again with the assurance of your pardon. In days of danger, hold your protecting hand over me. In mercy remember also my family and friends. Lighten the pain of parting for them. Be their trust concerning my well-being, and help them always to commend their cares to you in fervent prayer. Remind my family and me of the promise given to Jacob: "I am with you and will watch over you wherever you go." I ask this in the name of our Savior and Lord. Amen.

48. In Military Service

Almighty God, your protection is over us in every situation of our lives. I ask your blessing as I serve in the armed forces of our country. Guard my faith in Christ, the Savior. Permit no temptation to harm me in any way, but strengthen me for the experiences that I must face. Protect my body and health. Let nothing harmful happen to me as I carry out the work assigned to me in the service of my country. Especially if my duties call me into areas of great danger, be with me, O Lord, and protect me from evil. Help me as you have promised so that I may praise and glorify your saving name forever, through Jesus Christ our Lord. Amen.

49. Falling in Love

Gracious God, you created Adam and Eve and blessed them with perfect love for each other (Genesis 2:4-25). Thank you for this gift of love you have given. May this emotion find its root not in fleeting passion or harried hormones, which can so often lead to sin, but in the perfect love you give and demonstrated to us on the cross. May my love in this world follow your will, avoiding the selfishness of sin and living each day in love for you and then for others. Amen.

50. A Broken Heart

Precious Lord, "you are the God who sees me" and I know that you have heard of my misery and you hear my crying (Genesis 16:11,13; 21:17). My heart is broken. Please put it back together again. Help me remember that, even if everyone else stops loving me, I still have you. You'll never stop. Grant that your love would be enough for me all of my days. If there is some way for me to still be a blessing in the life of the person who has broken my heart, show me how. If not, send others to be a blessing in my place. Amen.

51. In Old Age

Our heavenly Father, we praise you for the multitude of blessings we have received and for the many happy memories that have come to us. Help us focus our attention on the good, the true, and the beautiful. We thank you for new friendships and old ones, for opportunities to serve, for the joys of home, and for the love of those who care. Though our physical strength decays, help us keep close to you so that our spiritual strength may be renewed day by day. Teach us to face our declining energies with patience. Lord God, our Father, take from us all fear of the future. As your dear children, we place our lives in your hands and, with faith and confidence, we walk the remaining paths of this life with you. Let your peace rule in our hearts today and through all of our tomorrows. We pray in the name of him who lived and died for us and now lives eternally, Jesus Christ our Lord. Amen.

52. Retirement

Your love for us never ends, eternal God. When we retire, keep us awake to your will for us. Give us energy to enjoy the world, to attend to neighbors whom busy people neglect, and to contribute wisely to the life of the church. If we can offer nothing but our prayers, remind us that our prayers are a useful work you want so that we may live always serving Jesus Christ, our hope and our true joy. Amen.

53. When Shut In

Dear Lord Jesus Christ, you came to die for my sins. You faithfully carried out every part of your heavenly Father's will. Now I have peace in the knowledge that your anger over my sins is gone. When my life is in turmoil because of health problems, calm my fears with the message of sins forgiven. When my life is tedious because of the sameness of my daily routine, point my eyes to the eternal excitement I will soon have in your presence. Bless all those who, like me, cannot come and go as we used to. Visit us daily through your Word, and let our minds and hearts leave our confines as we think about the many who need our prayers, in Jesus' name. Amen.

Prayers of Thanks and Praise

54. General Praise and Thanksgiving

As I look about me, dear Father in heaven, I see the work of your hands in the wonders of the universe, in the land and the sea, in the forests and the fields, and in the body you have given me. For all of these, receive my heartfelt thanks. Amen.

55. Thanks for the Word of God

Dear Lord, thank you for the light of your truth. I live in a world racing toward the day of judgment. So many people live in the darkness of error and unbelief. But in your Word, you have revealed the truth that leads to eternal life and you graciously led me to know my Savior. Keep me close to your Word so that the Holy Spirit may work through the gospel of your forgiveness. Amen.

56. Thanks for God's Creation

Lord God, open my eyes to the beauty of your created world. You made all things to nourish my life and to fill me with wonder and joy. Open my mouth to praise and thank you for your gifts. Amen.

57. Thanks for Blessings Received

For bountiful harvests, for the freedoms we enjoy, for family and friends, for all the blessings we receive, we give you thanks, O Lord. We truly are blessed to have a God who meets and exceeds our every need. It is amazing that we have been so blessed, especially when we consider that we don't deserve any of it. And yet, O Lord, you continue to amaze, inspire, and provide. As we are once again reminded of your goodness, lead us to give you the thanks you deserve. Amen.

58. Thanks for the Holy Angels' Protection

Lord of heavenly armies, I praise and thank you that you have sent your angels to guide me and guard me in all my ways. I thank you that they guard me from all the dangers around me that I can see. Even more so, I thank you that they guard me from the dangers I cannot see. Continue to send your angels until that day when they and I will worship you around your throne in heaven. Amen.

59. Thanks for My Health

Heavenly Father, I praise you for giving me my body, eyes, ears and all my members, my mind and all my abilities. Forgive me for easily taking this blessing for granted and for the times I have harmed my health by not using my body to your glory. Thank you for the days of good health you give to me. Help me to follow a healthy lifestyle in diet and exercise. May I always remember that my body is the temple of the Holy Spirit. Amen.

60. Thanks for Eyesight and Hearing

Lord Jesus, you yourself remind me, "Blessed are your eyes because they see, and your ears because they hear" (Matthew 13:16). What beauty my eyes behold as I look at the world you have created for me! How grateful I am for ears that detect and differentiate the many and various sounds with which you fill my life! Thank you most of all for opening my ears to hear of the wondrous things your Son has done for me and allowing me to behold with eyes of faith the great things he has done out of love for me. Amen.

61. Thanks for My Abilities

Lord God, you are the giver of every good gift. From your goodness I have received my body and soul, eyes, ears, and all my members, my mind, and all my abilities. Thank you. Help me to recognize my skills and talents as manifestations of your fatherly goodness. Send your Holy Spirit so that I may use all that I have in step with your gracious will. Increase my faith so that I look for opportunities to use the gifts you have given me for the good of my neighbor and for the praise of your name. Amen.

62. Praise for Preserving My Life Each Day

Heavenly Father, thank you for the gift of my life, for my heart that still beats, for my lungs that still breathe, and for the unknown accidents you keep me from each day. These are all daily gifts from your hand that I all too often take for granted. Forgive me for not caring for my body the way I ought. Thank you especially for daily preserving my spiritual life in Christ by your Holy Spirit. Help me to live to your glory and honor you with my body in thanks to you for preserving my life—physical and spiritual—each day. Amen.

63. Thanks for Food and Drink

All eyes look to you, gracious Lord, for nourishment in this fragile world. I depend on you and praise you for your wonderful works in supplying my food and drink each day. Give me a grateful heart for fields, farmers, grocers, and many more who serve me by helping to provide the abundant earthly blessings that come to me each day. Use these gifts to sustain me so that I can faithfully serve you and give you all glory with my body and mind. Amen.

64. Thanks for Clothing, Shoes, and Shelter

Dear heavenly Father, I confess that I have often been guilty of taking your gifts for granted. I enjoy the blessing of clothing, shoes, and shelter, without realizing that you have provided these blessings. When the clouds bring rain, I simply retreat to my house and let the water run off the roof while I remain warm and dry. When the chilling wind blows, I reach for a sweater to stay warm. My shoes keep my feet warm and dry. But I rarely stop to thank you for keeping me warm and comfortable. Such ingratitude only adds to the burden of guilt that makes me unworthy of these blessings. Forgive my guilt for Jesus' sake and help me to be grateful for warmth and shelter, remembering that you are the source of all my earthly blessings. In Jesus' name, I pray. Amen.

65. Thanks for My Means of Income

Thank you, dear heavenly Father, for giving me the opportunity and the ability to earn an income. You have provided my talent and training. You have led me to the place where I can use these gifts to provide useful service. You have given me the ability to provide food and shelter for myself and my family. I pray that you continue to provide these blessings. Preserve me from the struggles of unemployment. Preserve the system of Social Security that supports me in my old age. And keep me ever grateful for these blessings, lest I should fail to give you the praise you deserve. In Jesus' name, I ask it. Amen.

66. Thanks for My Parents

Dear heavenly Father, I believe that you have created me, giving me my body and soul, eyes, ears, and all my members, my mind and all my abilities. But I also know that you gave me these gifts through the man and woman who became my parents, who also nurtured and sheltered me through childhood. Help me to remember with gratitude the blessings I have received though them. Keep them in good health of body and soul so that when their life is over, they may receive the promised gift of eternal life through Jesus Christ, your Son, my Lord. Amen

67. Thanks for My Spouse

Lord, I am so grateful for my spouse. The one I love enriches my life in so many ways. At times I marvel at how similar we are. At other times I so much appreciate our differences. This was your great plan in marriage. You would enable two uniquely blessed individuals to be stronger, wiser, and more complete together as we find our strength in you. And that is what I am most thankful for. You, our Savior, have given me my best friend to walk heavenward with, who encourages and helps me walk closer to you. Continue to bless us as we journey on together in you, O Christ. Amen.

68. Thanks for My Children

Lord, on more than one occasion you have given the blessed command for us to "be fruitful and increase in number." The blessing of having and raising children is one of the greatest experiences you give us. I fully believe that "children are a heritage from the LORD, offspring a reward from him" (Psalm 127:3). Thank you for the gift of my children. Keep me mindful of the truth that you are their true Father. Help me to always view them as a blessing and to raise them according to your will. Amen.

69. Thanks for My Grandchildren

Lord God, heavenly Father, I want to express my gratefulness to you for my grandchildren, whom you have given to me as blessings on my earthly journey. Thank you for all the joy, love, and comfort they bring to my life. Help me to be a good example for them in my words and actions. May I remember to share with them how your grace and mercy has sustained me in this life and will sustain them too so that someday both they and I may stand together in heaven and give thanks to you for all you have done for us in our Savior Jesus Christ. Amen.

70. Thanks for My Country, Its Laws, and Its Freedoms

Lord, you reveal to us that all "authorities that exist have been established by [you]" (Romans 13:1). In humble and grateful appreciation I thank you for the joy of living in this country. Continue to rule and guide our leaders to uphold the freedoms that you granted our forefathers to establish for us. Especially safeguard our freedom of religion. How blessed we are to have laws and rules that protect our freedom to worship you. I clearly see your grace, mercy, and love in the rule you provide for our country. Please help me and my fellow citizens to appreciate what we have and to live lives of propriety and faithfulness to you, dear Lord. Amen.

71. Thanks for Those Who Protect My Country and Its Citizens

Almighty God, our Creator and protector, I approach your throne in gratitude for the many public servants who devote their lives to providing safety and security in this great land I call my home. Help me and every citizen to honor, respect, and support all who are employed in the armed forces, the fire departments, in medical professions, and the various police forces. Give these brave men and women both courage and compassion so that they might carry out their difficult tasks well. Keep them safe as they labor to serve and protect me and the citizens of this nation. Amen.

72. Praise for Good Weather

Lord of all creation, we praise and thank you for the good weather you graciously give us. You control the wind and the waves. You bring storms and sunlight. You guide the temperature and seasons and everything that brings life to this earth. Through these merciful gifts you bless us with good crops, healthy livestock, and all the conditions we need for health and life. May your kind providence lead us to work diligently in all our callings, serve our neighbors faithfully, and enjoy the rest and recreation that good weather provides. Amen.

73. Thanks for Good Friends

Lord Jesus Christ, you told the disciples that they were no longer slaves but friends (John 15:13-15). Thank you for the gift of friendship: for those people who share our joys and sorrows, in whom we confide, and through whom you console and comfort us. Strengthen these relationships as we live in the love you so freely gave to us as our greatest friend! Amen.

74. Thanks for Happy Memories

Lord of heaven, though here on earth we have trials and troubles of all kinds, in your love and mercy you allow your people times of joy and bless our days with both thrilling experiences and quiet times to delight in the company of those we love. Though

there is much error and evil in my life that I prefer to forget,
I thank you for the rich and repeating gift of the memories of
the many joys, blessed days, and love. In your mercy, I pray for
Jesus' sake that they remain always ready and vivid in my heart
and mind. Amen.

75. Praise for Being So Good and Merciful to Me

Gracious Lord Jesus, you have come that I may have life and
live it to the full. In your mercy, I have pardon for sin and eternal
life. I am overwhelmed by the steady shower of spiritual and
material blessings that flows to me from your great goodness.
You have provided for my needs and, often, for my wants. Grant
me a heart so grateful that I am not content merely to enjoy your
blessings but that, as an expression of my thanks, I may share
your gifts to enrich the lives of others and to help meet their
needs. Amen.

76. Praise for My Eternal Election in Christ

Heavenly Father, praise be to you for your merciful love in
Christ that chose me even before the world began. It was your
pleasure and plan from all eternity that I should be your own for
all eternity, holy and blameless in your sight (Ephesians 1:4-6).
I glorify you for sending your Son to carry out my salvation.
I thank you for calling me through your Word and justifying
me by grace through faith in Jesus Christ. Let your eternal plan
comfort me in all trials and reassure me of my eternal inheritance
that you have promised and sealed in me with your Holy Spirit
(Ephesians 1:13,14), so that no one can ever snatch me out of
your hand (John 10:27-29). In Jesus' name I pray. Amen.

77. Praise for Christ's Incarnation

Lord Jesus, Word made flesh, how wonderful is your incarnation
to me. You made yourself nothing for me so that I could have
everything in you. You became a man here in time so that I could
enjoy eternity with God. You, the Son of God, became the Son
of Man so that I could become a child of God. You came down
in the weakness of my flesh so that I could find strength in your

unfailing presence. I praise you, my dear brother, Jesus Christ, because you are not ashamed to call us your brothers and sisters (Hebrews 2:11). In your name I pray. Amen.

78. Praise for Christ's Victorious Descent Into Hell

Lord Jesus, your perfect life and innocent death paid the all-sufficient price for the sins of the world. You descended into hell to proclaim your victory there (1 Peter 3:19) and to prove that you had triumphed over Satan and his angels (Colossians 2:15). You have shut hell and opened heaven to me and all believers. Let your victory for me strengthen my heart and defend me against my enemies all the days of my life. Glory, praise, and honor be to you now and forever. Amen.

79. Praise for Redeeming Me

Dearest owner of my body and soul, for 33 years you labored in order to win me as your own. You endured homelessness. You often lost sleep to pray for more strength. You let men abuse and crucify you. And it was all to pay my bride-price and walk me down the aisle. It was all to buy me away from the slaughterhouse and lead me into your own green pastures. How could I be worth so much to you? Why should you be so devoted to me? What makes me a treasure in your eyes? Let me be yours forever! (CW 596:1) Amen.

80. Thanks for the Blood of Jesus

Lord Jesus, how precious is your blood that you poured out on the cross to reconcile the whole world to yourself (1 Peter 1:18,19; Colossians 1:20)! With your own blood you purchased the church of God from every nation on earth (Acts 20:28; Revelation 5:9). With your own blood you now purify me from all sin (1 John 1:7). Through your own blood I now triumph over Satan, my accuser, whom you have defeated (Revelation 12:10,11). Because no other price than your holy and innocent blood could have redeemed me, I offer my thanks and praise for your boundless mercy and love. In your name I pray. Amen.

81. Thanks for Complete Forgiveness

The hymn writer beautifully proclaimed, "My sin, not in part, but the whole, is nailed to the cross, and I bear it no more" (CWS 760). Thank you for complete forgiveness! Since you fully paid the price for the sins of the whole world, it means you fully paid the price for my sins too. Your complete forgiveness means I can have complete comfort, complete confidence in your love, and complete joy as I wait for the day my life is completed and you take me home to live with you in paradise. Amen.

82. Thanks for Freedom From Sin's Power

Lord God, I was enslaved to my sin until this truth set me free (John 8:32): through faith in Jesus Christ I am no longer condemned for my sin (Romans 8:1). Your Son took on flesh to free me from this body of sin and death. Now death has lost its sting (1 Corinthians 15:55,56), the father of lies cannot deceive me (John 8:44), and sin does not rule over me anymore (Romans 6:6,7). Thanks and praise be to you for rescuing me from my sin and giving me victory through your Son, my Lord Jesus Christ. In his name, I pray. Amen.

83. Thanks for Freedom From Death's Power

Risen Lord Jesus, I see the power of death all around me. It steals my loved ones, and it hangs over me like a tarp because I know my time is coming someday. I pray that you would take me back to the empty tomb to hear again the words of the angel telling me that you are alive. I thank and praise you for your resurrection, for that is what has freed me from death's power. Help me to rejoice in your resurrection and to live every day in freedom from death's power. Amen.

84. Thanks for Freedom From Satan's Power

Lord Jesus Christ, you already defeated Satan in your life and work. Thank you. As your gospel spreads, his work is constantly frustrated and destroyed. Thank you. Thank you for strengthening us with your Word so that we may know your will and do it. When tempted, help us to defend ourselves as you did by telling Satan "Away from me!" and by answering each temptation with the Word of God. Thank you for your continuing help to reject Satan's empty claim that your commands are burdensome. Thank you for helping us follow your call to freedom and happiness, as we grow closer to you. Amen.

85. Thanks for the Holy Spirit

Lord Jesus, before you ascended into heaven, you promised to send your Holy Spirit to be my Counselor. Thank you for keeping your promise and filling me with his presence. If it weren't for him and his work, I wouldn't be able to trust in you. In connecting me to you, what wonderful blessings flow from your heart into mine: love, joy, peace, patience, kindness, goodness, gentleness, faithfulness, and self-control. Grant me a rich measure of your Spirit's presence as I seek to bear abundant fruit for your glory with my life! Amen.

86. Thanks for Bringing Me to the Faith

Dear life-giving Holy Spirit, I am eternally grateful for the amazing miracle you have worked in my heart through your powerful gospel. Forgive me for the times I've taken this gift for granted or have treated it as a small thing. By the ongoing comfort of pardon from all sin through the merit of Jesus, continue to strengthen this faith you have given until faith becomes sight in heaven. In Jesus' name. Amen.

87. Praise for Gathering the Holy Christian Church From All Nations

Praise to you, O Lord, for the Great Commission to "make disciples of all nations" (Matthew 28:19). The gospel message that we share proclaims salvation to all people through your Son, Jesus Christ. I thank you for giving us authority to tell everyone we know that their sins have been forgiven through the suffering and death of your Son. Lord, your plan is for all believers in Jesus to form one body, one church. Today, Christians gather in many places in the world to praise your holy name. Jesus, keep me and all believers strong in faith until you gather us all to be with you in heavenly glory. Amen.

88. Thanks for My Pastor

Gracious Lord, you place your precious gospel in fragile jars of clay and send these, your representatives, to proclaim the Word and administer the sacraments in your kingdom. Thank you for Pastor _____, whom you called to serve me and the members of _____ congregation. Keep him faithful to the tasks of correcting, encouraging, rebuking, and training the saints in this place with your Holy Scriptures. Help me show appreciation for my pastor as I support him with prayers and encouragement, and regular attendance in Bible class and worship. Amen.

89. Thanks for the Knowledge That Death Is But a Sleep

Lord Jesus, you are the conqueror of death. Death entered this world because of our sin (Romans 5:12), but we now praise you for defeating death and giving us the victory of life through your own life, death, and resurrection. Death has lost its sting and is now only as terrifying to us as sleep is. When we close our eyes at death and wake in heaven, we will be safe and have peaceful rest in paradise. When you wake our bodies on the Last Day, we will rise refreshed and renewed through the power of your resurrection. Thanks be to you now and forever, Lord of life. Amen.

90. Thanks for the Hope of a Bodily Resurrection

Jesus Christ, my resurrected Lord, you have redeemed me as one person with both soul and body. Just as your Word assures me that my soul has been saved eternally through your saving work, so your Word promises that my body, even though it will die and decay, will be raised to new life and transformed to be like your glorious body (Philippians 3:21). For this sure and certain hope, I give you all my thanks and praise. Grant me patience to wait with hope for that day when death will be destroyed (1 Corinthians 15:26) and sin's devastating effects on my body will vanish forever. In your name, I pray. Amen.

91. Thanks for All the Saints

Everlasting God, the generations rise and pass away before you. You are the strength of those who labor; you are the rest of the blessed dead. We rejoice in the company of your saints. We remember all who have lived in faith, all who have died in the peace of forgiveness, and especially those most dear to us who rest in you. When our end comes, grant us a place with those who have trusted in you and have striven to do your holy will. With the church on earth and the church in heaven, we ascribe all honor and glory to your name, now and forever. Amen.

92. Thanks for Answers to Prayer

Thank you, my always-listening God, my ever-generous Father! So many nights I have asked you to keep me, so many mornings I have commended my life into your hands, and here I am today. I could never list all the ways you have opened when I knocked, given what I asked, and led me to find what I sought in your Son Jesus' name (Matthew 7:7,8). How pleasant it is to have daily access to your throne! No one is as dependable as you. You truly have satisfied my desires with good things (Psalm 103:5). I don't ever want to stop thanking you. Amen.

93. Thanks for My Baptism

Most merciful God, with the sprinkling of water in connection with your Word, you adopted me into your family of believers. Thank you for pouring upon me the benefits of Christ's death and resurrection. I am your forgiven child. What joy fills my heart to belong to your family of believers! Help me remember my baptism and live under the blessings of your grace all my life. Amen.

94. Thanks for Holy Communion

Generous Lord God, you graciously feed my physical body with the bounties of the earth, but you do not neglect to feed my soul.

Thank you for the spiritual food and drink of Jesus' body and blood given to me with the unleavened bread and the grape wine in the Lord's Supper. Do not let me despise this precious meal, but rather enjoy it regularly with my fellow Christians, for the strengthening of my faith and for the assurance of eternal peace in your presence. Amen.

95. Praise for the Real Presence of Christ's Body and Blood in Communion

Lord of the Exodus, when you passed through the land to strike down the Egyptians, you saw the Passover lambs' blood painted on the Israelites' doorframes and you passed over them, not permitting the destroyer to enter (Exodus 12:23). You graciously give me your Son's very body and blood, not just for on my doorframe but in my own unworthy mouth. I know you will see it and keep the destroyer away from me. Yes, this is my deliverance, my assurance against every plague, and my joy in the face of all injustice. Thank you for the body and the blood! Amen.

96. Praise for Giving Human Beings the Authority to Forgive Sins

My great assurance, my heart's true rest, I praise you for placing the promise of forgiveness into the mouths of my pastor and my fellow Christians. When I want to know my sins are taken away, I don't need some ladder or telephone line up into heaven. Any Christian can tell me, and it's as sure as hearing your own voice through a hole in the sky, as sure as the thunder-peal pronouncements from Mount Sinai, as sure as if I stood under Christ's cross and heard him say, "I do this for you." You are so kind, so considerate of my doubt-prone mind. Amen.

97. Thanks for Medical Caregivers, When Hospitalized

Dear Father, we thank you for life and for every gift of your love. We thank you for this hospital and for all the caregivers. O Great Physician, may your hand bring continued healing. As you bring health and strength, so give peace of mind and heart. Sustain our faith with your promises of forgiveness and life through Jesus Christ our Lord. Amen.

98. Thanks for Medical Technology, When Hospitalized

Mighty and merciful God, you sent Jesus Christ to heal broken lives. We praise you also for sending healing through medical technology and those in the medical profession. Grant wholeness and restoration of health as we pray for those who are ill in body or mind, who long for your healing touch. Make the weak strong, the sick healthy, the broken whole, and make those who serve them agents of your love. Then all will be renewed in vigor to point to the risen Christ, who conquered death that we might live eternally. Amen.

Prayers for the Family

99. For Single Christians

Lord Jesus, you are the example for single people of all times.
Give the single people in our midst the strength to live a
Christian life. Let encouragement from family and friends
sustain them when days are lonely. Give them joy in lives of
service to you. When the pressures of the world and sinful
society seem overpowering, remind them that you are with
them always. Fortify them against all temptations. Reassure
them through your promises that you know all things and are
directing their lives in your wisdom and love. Amen.

100. That God Would Give Me a Godly Spouse

Almighty God, in the beginning you made us male and female.
In your wisdom, you still decide the exact time and place that
people live. Yet, I'm still alone. Forgive me for the times I haven't
been content with trusting your plan for my life. As I search for a
godly spouse, help me to grow and mature so that I can, in turn,
be a godly blessing. Grant me peace as I trust the Good Shepherd
who laid down his life for me. Keep my heart always focused on
heaven so that I do not miss out on your greatest blessings as I
seek this one. If it is your will, grant me someone whom I may
love as Christ loved me. Amen.

101. Before Proposing Marriage

Gracious God, abounding in love, I thank you for bringing this
special woman into my life. I am excited and nervous. Please
let this moment be as beautiful for her as I am hoping it will be.
Bless us as we make our wedding plans. Help us live decent
and pure lives until our wedding. Keep us prayerful and careful
so that the time of our engagement will be blemished neither
by wedding worries nor fleshly lusts. Strengthen our faith and
communication through our premarital studies in your Word.
Let our wedding and our marriage always put you first. Amen.

102. For Those About to Be Married

Lord God, you created man and woman in your image, and it pleased you to unite them as one in holy matrimony. You have greatly honored marriage by making it a symbol of the spiritual union between Christ and his bride, the church. Grant that _____ and _____ may reflect this perfect love and commitment in their marriage all the days of their lives. Make their home your temple, and make their marriage a testimony to others so that your name is glorified among us. Amen.

103. Marriage

Heavenly Savior, as you have instituted and blessed marriage, so also help us who are married to keep you ever with us. Forgive us those times when we let anger, distrust, unhappiness, or lack of devotion harm our relationships. Teach us to turn to you and to talk to each other to get through difficult times. Let your love for us show through us to each other. Strengthen us and keep us together with you in love all our days. Amen.

104. At the Anniversary of a Marriage

Triune God, as _____ and _____ celebrate their _____ wedding anniversary, accept our heartfelt thanks for all the blessings they have received. As companions on the journey through life, they have loved, consoled, and supported each other, but most important, they have grown closer to you. By your grace they have maintained a Christian home and raised their children in the training and instruction of the Lord. They have learned forgiveness and unconditional love from you. Your Word has been a lamp to their feet and a light for their path. Keep them committed to each other and to you. Continue to supply their earthly needs according to your will. Give them joy in the years to come, through Jesus Christ our Lord. Amen.

105. For a Married Couple

O God of tenderness and strength, bless our home and our love, our comings and our goings. Keep us from growing weary in doing good, and sustain us in the hour of trouble. Help us deal tenderly with each other, and knit our lives together in love for you and each other. Amen.

106. For Good Communication in Marriage

Loving Lord Jesus, I praise you for your institution of marriage. Forgive me for the times I have not patiently listened to my spouse. Thank you for a spirit of self-giving love, which your Holy Spirit works in my heart. Cause that spirit to flourish in me. Keep me from being silent when I need to speak. Help me always to speak the truth in love. Amen.

107. After an Argument Between Husband and Wife

Husband: Jesus Christ, forgive my selfishness and pride. I have failed to love my wife as you loved the church. My anger, arrogance, and insistence on my way have created tension with my wife. May I find assurance of forgiveness for my sin in your Word and my baptism. Help me to confess my failure to my wife and strengthen me to correct my sinful words and actions. May I speak to my wife in a way that reflects the love I ought to have for her—a love that sacrifices my desires for her good. Amen.

Wife: Jesus Christ, forgive my selfishness and pride. I have failed to respect my husband as the church respects you. My desire for what I want has led to quarreling instead of building up my husband. May I find assurance of forgiveness for my sin in your Word and my baptism. Help me to confess my failure to my husband and strengthen me to correct my sinful words and actions. May I speak to my husband in a way that reflects the respect I ought to have for him—a respect that sees the good you give me through him. Amen.

108. After I Have Been Inconsiderate Toward My Spouse

Lord, you have made the husband and wife relationship to be unique and incredibly special. You tell us that when two individuals get married they become one flesh. Even though you have made us one, at times I am still inconsiderate toward my spouse. Forgive me for thoughtless words and selfish actions. Make me mindful of my words before I speak and thoughtful of my actions before I act. By your Spirit, give me the strength to be a blessing to my spouse rather than a source of pain and frustration. Amen.

109. When the Marriage Is in Trouble

Heavenly Father, when your creation was still perfect, you instituted marriage as a blessing to your people. But sin has tainted our marriage. Forgive us, Lord, for all the ways we've sinned against you and hurt each other. Help us also to forgive each other as you forgive all sin through Jesus' blood. Help us, Lord, to put aside our anger and seek good counsel through your Word, through your church, and through Christian counselors so that we may continue to selflessly serve you as we selflessly serve each other. In the name of Jesus we pray. Amen.

110. That Nothing Would Hinder the Couple's Prayers

Holy Lord, consecrate our ears to listen to each other. Consecrate our hands to serve each other. Consecrate our feet so that we might patiently stay by each other's side. Consecrate our mouths to speak to each other only in love and to speak to you in unceasing prayer. Let no sinful anger or quarreling defile our marriage, lest even the slightest resentment get in the way of these our prayers to you. Amen.

111. Renewing Marriage Promises

O almighty God, most merciful Father, we praise you for the loving-kindness and tender mercies which you have bestowed on _____ and _____, providing for them by your goodness, defending them by your power, and guiding them by your mercy. Accept the sacrifice of thanksgiving that they offer to you, and give ear to their humble request. Help them to fulfill the promises they have renewed here today and to reflect your steadfast love in their love for each other. Be their refuge and strength in every infirmity of body and soul. Use their family and friends to support them in difficult days, that their love for each other may continue to grow as long as they live. Let them know the peace of your Holy Spirit, and keep them faithful to you and to each other until the day when they shall enjoy the eternal pleasures of your kingdom, through Jesus Christ, your Son, our Lord. Amen.

112. When a Spouse Is Ill

It is hard to watch my spouse suffer from this illness, dear Jesus. You healed so many people during your time on earth; please heal my spouse too. In the meantime, help me know how best to support my spouse, how best to put my other responsibilities on hold to give my spouse extra time, and what words to say to keep my spouse trusting in you. Have mercy, Lord. Amen.

113. At a Spouse's Death

O ever-blessed God, the peace of the world and the joy of your people, uphold your servant. Grant me firm faith in your promise, "Do not fear, for I have redeemed you; I have summoned you by name; you are mine" (Isaiah 43:1). Put such a spirit of trust in me, that all fear and foreboding will be cast out and that calm assurance may rule my thoughts and impulses. Let quietness of spirit and confidence in your loving presence rule my life. Focus my eyes on the empty tomb of your Son so that I may there find hope and peace. Into your loving care I commend myself, through Jesus Christ our Lord. Amen.

114. After My Spouse Has Been Unfaithful

Blessed Jesus, hear my prayer and take away my hurt and frustration. Be with me and my spouse. If it is your will, help us regain our love for each other through our love for you. I look to your perfect love, knowing you will not forsake me or my spouse. Please forgive the person my spouse cheated with. Help me and my beloved to seek your forgiveness always. Send your Holy Spirit to heal us both. My spouse has broken our marriage, which you intended and commanded to last all life long (Matthew 19:1-6). Now what? Will our marriage be restored? Guide us both. Never stop. I ask this in Jesus' name. Amen.

115. After a Divorce

So many times I prayed for my marriage. Did you not look on those prayers with favor, Lord? I know that I must not blame you for the sins that have ruined this marriage. But it is a mess. It's so awful compared to what I imagined when we made our vows before you on our wedding day. Change my heart—toward you, toward my ex, and toward my situation. Heal the grief that this divorce has caused the rest of our family. Show us how you are working all of this toward some good end. Amen.

116. A Parent's Prayer

Gracious Father in heaven, we thank you for the blessing of children. Let our manner with our children reflect the love you have toward us. Grant us the patience and ability to meet their needs. Give us the wisdom to use your Word effectively as the guide for our personal lives and in the instruction of our children. Grant all parents a measure of love that will not diminish under the burdens of this life. As you are always ready to forgive and to restore us, let us learn to exercise discipline in love, with a readiness to forgive. We ask this in Jesus' name. Amen.

117. For Fathers

Heavenly Father, bless all earthly fathers as they seek to fulfill the calling you have entrusted to them. Give them loving hearts and sound judgment to exercise godly family leadership. May they daily take to heart your admonition not to discourage or embitter their children by treating them harshly or unfairly. Help them, instead, to bring up their children in the training and instruction of the Lord. In loving Christian fathers, may children see reflections of you, the Father whose love for us is perfect and complete. Amen.

118. For Mothers

Heavenly Father, you are the source of life, wisdom, and all good things. Look with favor on all mothers who have given life to their children and who nurture them with loving concern and faithful instruction. May their children honor them and call them blessed.

When they become weary, sustain them with physical and spiritual rest. Hear us for the sake of your Son, Jesus, who cared for his earthly mother and in whom you are well pleased. Amen.

119. Expecting a Child

O Lord our God, Creator of all that exists, we thank you for the joy of knowing new life has begun and for the privilege of sharing with you in your continuing creation. In your mercy grant that these blessings may continue to us and to our children's children so that generations yet unborn may praise your holy name; through Jesus Christ our Lord. Amen.

120. Facing Infertility

Heavenly Father, we, your dear children, cry out to you with pain and sorrow because you have not blessed us with the gift of a child. In this time of uncertainty, comfort us with the greatest gift you could ever give to us: your only Son, Jesus Christ. If it is not your good pleasure for us to carry a child in our arms, enable us to always carry your Son in our hearts through faith so that his abiding presence would continually fill this aching void and bring peace to our longing hearts. Grant us grace and strength to persevere as husband and wife together in your dear Son, in whose name we pray. Amen.

121. After a Stillbirth or Miscarriage

Almighty and eternal God, our hopes have been turned to sorrow. You gave, and you have taken away. As the heavens are higher than the earth, so are your ways higher than our ways and your thoughts higher than our thoughts (Isaiah 55:8,9). Help us, Father, also in this time of sadness to trust in you. Strengthen our faith and comfort us, whose life you have allowed sorrow to enter. Teach us to depend on your boundless mercy and to trust that our little one has been invited into the arms of your Son. Grant that all of us may also come at last into the heavenly kingdom of Jesus Christ our Lord, who lives and reigns with you and the Holy Spirit, one God, now and forever. Amen.

122. Before Childbirth

Gracious Father in Christ, I know that you are concerned about your children in all of their needs. Therefore, I place myself and my child into your compassionate and almighty care. I implore you, strengthen me with the assurance that you will watch over me throughout the time of my labor. Support me by your almighty power as the time of my delivery draws near. Lead me to place myself and my unborn child into your loving hands. If it is your will, gladden my heart with the gift of a healthy child so that I may praise and glorify you for the great privilege of having been your instrument in the creation of a new life. In Jesus' name I ask this. Amen.

123. At the Birth of a Child

We thank you, Father, for the gift of life and for your power and promises that preserve life. We thank you still more for having sent Jesus to adopt this child into your family and for sending the Spirit in Baptism to renew your image in *him*. Help us parents to be models of your love. Make your church a fellowship of encouragement and admonition to foster growth and godliness in *him*. We ask this in the name of Jesus, who welcomes little children. Amen.

124. Thanksgiving for Protecting a Mother Through Childbirth

Dear Father in heaven, accept my heartfelt thanks for watching over me during my time of labor and pain and for granting me the privilege and joy of bringing a new life into this world. Let me never forget, O Lord, that my child is a miracle of your creative hand—that *he* is not mere flesh of my flesh but a person redeemed by the precious blood of Jesus our Savior. Grant me the grace to recognize clearly the great responsibility you have bestowed on me in giving me this child, and help me to train *him* in the way that leads to everlasting life, through Jesus Christ our Lord. Amen.

125. Thanksgiving for a Child's Baptism

Gracious God, I marvel not only at your ability to give life to this child's body but also at the special gift of life you have given to *his* soul through the waters of Baptism. Help me to rejoice that you have connected this child to the death and resurrection of Jesus. Allow *his* baptism to assure *him* often that you have washed *him* clean and applied the perfect life of Jesus to *him*, and right now you consider *him* to be your child. Encourage this child with the promises you have made and the promises you keep in Baptism. Amen.

126. When I Find Out My Child Has Special Needs

Dear Lord, Creator and giver of life, you know everything I'm thinking right now: How will my child cope, what will the other kids say, and how will I manage? You also know all of the answers. Give me the courage to challenge the limits of these special needs. But most of all, give me an understanding of what my child is going through and the patience to cope with all that will come from this. Remind me that this child is a special gift from you and that you will surely give me the strength to love and care for *him*. Amen.

127. When the Baby Isn't Sleeping Well

Lord, I need patience! My little child, a blessing from you, is having a difficult time sleeping and so am I. If it is your will, help this rough patch pass quickly and allow my baby and me to find peaceful rest. Give us calm nights and rested minds and bodies. Remind us that you never slumber or sleep and are watching over us. When the dawn comes, reassure me that you are with me and will give me the necessary stamina and strength to be a loving parent, even when I'm tired. Amen.

128. When a Child Starts to Crawl and Explore

Heavenly Father, you have designed the development of human life in its many stages. You have allowed this child to begin to experience life in this world with movement. May you be with *him* everywhere *he* goes all the days of *his* life. Keep *him* safe in your care now and along every step of *his* development. May these first movements be the first steps in a journey that leads to the eternal life in glory that Jesus has won, for he has come to live and move among us and right now lives as our victorious Savior. Amen.

129. For Patience With Whiny Children

Holy Spirit, you pour out the gifts of love, joy, peace, patience, kindness, goodness, faithfulness, gentleness, and self-control upon your people (Galatians 5:22,23). Today my patience is being put to the test as the children whine. Help me to flee to the cross for forgiveness, understanding that I have often complained, nagged, whimpered, and whined to you when life didn't follow my will. In your love, which focuses me on Jesus' perfect life and sacrificial death, pour out your gifts so that I might better love the children with whom you have blessed me. Amen.

130. Thanksgiving for a Child's Confirmation

Lord, you give us children as a precious blessing. In love you direct us to train them in your Word. As my child stands before your altar to make promises for confirmation, my heart overflows with thankfulness. I am thankful that you have brought my child to saving faith in Jesus. I am thankful that you have preserved and grown my child in faith through your Word. I am thankful that you have brought my child to desire to publicly confess that faith before the congregation. May *his* confirmation be but the beginning of an ever-increasing trust in you. Amen.

131. At the Placement of an Adopted Child

Heavenly Father, we thank you that you have answered our earnest prayers for the gift of a child. Grant us wisdom and dedication to care for *his* needs, and daily strengthen the bond of love between us and _____. Especially lead us to instruct *him* in your saving Word and bring *him* to your sacrament(s) so that *he* may be and remain your child. Sustain and encourage this family in the years to come, and move us to praise you again and again for uniting us in one family. We pray in Jesus' name. Amen.

132. For Wisdom in Training Up Children

Dear all-wise and generous Father, I thank you for giving me the privilege of being a mirror that reflects your love to the children you've entrusted to my care. I am often overwhelmed by the serious responsibility and changing nature of this task. Grant me wisdom from your Spirit through your Word so that I might carry out this task in a way that is pleasing to you and beneficial to these precious children. Help me to train them to trust and love you above all. I pray in Jesus' name. Amen.

133. When a Child Is Misbehaving

I cannot carry this child to adulthood by myself; the burden is too heavy for me, Lord (Numbers 11:14). I am troubled by my child's misbehavior. Pour out your Holy Spirit upon both me and my child. Be my eyes so that I might see how to respond, how to keep my patience, and how to communicate to my child the seriousness of this sin and the wonder of your forgiveness. Yes, please do forgive my child. Lead my child to repentance. Help my child, who is your child too through Baptism, to live not for self but humbly and always for you. Amen.

134. When My Children Don't Want to Do Their Homework or Chores

Heavenly Father, children are a heritage from you (Psalm 127:3)! Help me to treasure this truth always, especially when parenting is difficult and my children are uncooperative. Grant me a heart to love them, not only when they are cooperative but even when they are obstinate and disobedient. Use me to help lovingly restore in them a desire to listen and learn, to grow in willing obedience, in godly service, and in developing the gifts that you have entrusted to them. Amen.

135. After Disciplining a Child

Unchanging God, forgive me whatever sins have tainted my efforts to discipline my child. I know that, in my frustration, I do not always trust you as I should or represent you to my child in the completely holy way that I should (Numbers 20:12). Despite my sins, let this discipline bear good fruit, even a "harvest of righteousness and peace" in my child's life (Hebrews 12:11). Please give me the best words to reassure my child that *he* is loved and that you love *him* too. Help *him* to keep maturing and gaining wisdom until *he* knows well how to turn away from every reckless path. Amen.

136. For a Godly Spouse for My Child

Heavenly Father, before any single day of my *son's* life came to be, you knew them all. Please bless *his* future and allow *him* to grow into a *man* who knows and serves you in all *he* does. Please provide a godly spouse for *him* so that *he* might have a companion for this earthly pilgrimage. Provide someone to help *him* accomplish the work you allow *him* to do, someone who will help *him* grow in the grace you have given in Christ so that together one day, both my child and *his* future spouse may praise you in the glory of heaven. Amen.

137. Before a Child's First Date

God of love, Lord of all growing up, you already know how this first date will go, how my child's date will treat *him,* and how significant this relationship will be to my child as time goes on. Help my child to be respectful of *his* date. Help *him* remember your commandments and watch *him*self closely so that *he* does not forget that you are there with *him* or forget how you would have *him* act (Deuteronomy 4:9). Let these young people have a fun time, enjoy each other's company, and be caring Christian friends to each other. Amen.

138. Before a Child's Wedding

Dear faithful Father, you have kept all of your promises in your Word to save us and be with us. I will soon hear my child promise to love, cherish, and be faithful to another for a lifetime. I am thankful you have given my child a partner for this life and ask you to help my child honor the promises soon to be made before you. Strengthen me as well during this special day as I say good-bye, in a way, to my child and let go of this child to a new family. Remind me and my child of your abiding presence each day in the future and of your continued strength for our lives. In your Son's saving name. Amen.

139. For a Sick Child

O Father of our Lord Jesus Christ, who loved little children and took them in his arms, hear our prayer. In your infinite goodness look down on _____, your dear child. Work in this place and in this child's body with the healing power that comes from your creative will. Cause us to have greater faith and trust in you. Bless all that is being done to bring a restoration of health. In Jesus' name, we pray. Amen.

140. When a Child Is Gravely Ill

Heavenly Father, to whom all children are dear, we come to you because our hearts are bowed down with anxiety for our sick child. In response to your gracious invitation and promise— "Call upon me in the day of trouble; I will deliver you"—we implore you mercifully to ease *his* suffering and, if it is your will, to restore *him* to health again. Bless those who attend to his needs. Grant to us who watch and wait the sustaining comfort that you will do what is best both for us and for *him*. We ask this in the name of our Savior Jesus Christ, by whose suffering and death the door of heaven has been opened to our prayers. Amen.

141. When a Child Is Near Death

Dear Father, in the midst of divine and human love, this child was born. You gave *him* to us. You love *him* even as we do. In confidence and trust, we give *him* back to you. We know that *he* is yours. As we struggle with our doubts, speak peace to our hearts. Take from us all bitterness and mistrust. Cause us to be aware that we are your children. Although we do not know the answer to many of life's difficult questions, we do know that we live in your love. We confidently yield ourselves to you, because you have given your very self to us through Jesus, who loves all children. Amen.

142. At a Small Child's Death

O Lord, our God, your ways are often hidden, unsearchable, and beyond our understanding. For reasons we cannot comprehend, you have turned our joyful hopes into sadness. We know, dear Lord, that your ways are loving and wise. But we are often confused and fearful. Help us in our sorrow to bow humbly before your will. Comfort us with your life-giving promise that in all things, you are working for our good. Amen.

143. At an Older Child's Death

Eternal God, you gave _____ a new birth in Baptism and entrusted *him* to us for a time that seems too short. As we thank you for the life we shared, help us now to remember that *he* is with you in heavenly glory. Bring us all to that day when we shall stand in your presence with all your saints in light eternal, through Jesus Christ our Lord. Amen.

144. For a Sick Family Member

O God, our ever-present help in trouble, we implore your mercy in behalf of our loved one who is ill. Let the light and warmth of your grace shine on *him*. Drive the shadows of doubt and fear from *his* heart through the sure knowledge that *he* is your forgiven child through Christ and that *his* sickness, under your fatherly direction, is sent for *his* eternal good. Abide with *him* and with us as we journey through this world of sin and sorrow until, by your grace, we enter the joy and glory of heaven. Through Jesus Christ our Lord. Amen.

145. When a Family Member Is Gravely Ill

Heavenly Father, in your great wisdom and concern for your redeemed children, you sometimes permit heavy affliction to come upon them. You have assured us in your Holy Word that

"the Lord disciplines the one he loves" (Hebrews 12:6). So we
know that every affliction is intended for our eternal good.
This, then, we know is also the purpose of the serious illness
that rests on our loved one. We implore you, ease the burden of
his suffering. If it is your will, let this sickness pass from *him* or
grant *him* the needed strength to bear it. Fill *his* heart, we pray,
with the assurance that *he* is your beloved child through Jesus,
our Lord and Savior, in whose name we boldly and confidently
ask this blessing. Amen.

146. At a Loved One's Death

Almighty God, source of all mercy and giver of all comfort,
deal graciously, we pray, with us who mourn so that, casting all
our sorrow on you, we may know the consolation of your love
through your Son, Jesus Christ, our Lord. Amen.

147. At a Loved One's Death—When Death Means the Pain Is Over

We thank you, Lord Jesus Christ, that you have taken
_____ away from distress and brought *him* into eternal
rest. We say with Job, "The LORD gave and the LORD has taken
away; may the name of the LORD be praised" (1:21). Help us find
comfort through the realization that we have not lost *him* but
have only sent *him* before us to heaven. Let this death remind
us to be ready at all times to follow your call to depart from this
world to the joys of the life to come. Through Jesus Christ our
Lord. Amen.

148. Upon a Sudden Death

Lord God, by a sudden death you have called to yourself our
beloved *brother*. We humble ourselves under your holy will and
revere your ways, which are not always our ways. We thank you
that in your fatherly love you gave _____ your merciful
guidance and constant blessing in body and soul throughout
his life. Let your Holy Word comfort all of us who feel sorrow
because of this death. Strengthen us with the assurance that in
all things, you are still at work in truth and love. Teach us to

number our days. Help us seek the things that are above so that we may at last appear before your presence in peace and joy, through Jesus Christ our Lord. Amen.

149. Upon a Suicide

Gracious teacher, compassionate Lord, I have more questions than answers, and my heart is breaking. Someone near and dear has, in desperation, taken *his* own life. Have mercy on all those who love *him* and grant relief both from the grief of sudden loss and the guilt of self-recrimination and regret. Please forgive us for all the ways that we sinned against *him*; help us to understand so that we may learn from this and share what we have learned; and give us strength, peace, and wisdom for the difficult days ahead. I cling to your cross for comfort. Amen.

150. Upon a Murder

Why does this have to be? Where were the guardian angels? Why didn't you send someone to stop it? O Lord, this tremendous guilty deed, this shedding of innocent blood (Deuteronomy 21:7-9)—how could you bear to see it? My loved one is dead. Slain. Taken away. I'm not even sure what to pray. It hurts so much. It is so wrong. I cannot understand you. Don't let me lose my faith in you. I know my loved one, your redeemed child, is still alive to you, for to you "all are alive" (Luke 20:38). Let this and all your other gospel comforts give my family peace. Amen.

151. Upon a Death Under Troubling Circumstances

Dear Lord, only you know when and how we will die (1 Samuel 2:6; James 4:13-15). You direct us to be ready at any time for death, trusting you to take us to be with you in heaven. Please help us trust you now. Why did our loved one have to die like this? Why couldn't it be more peaceful? Why couldn't *he* have had more time to prepare? Help us believe that you were prepared for this day of evil. Help us pray submissively like Jesus did in Gethsemane, pondering his own troubling death: "Your will be done," Lord (Matthew 26:42). Our minds are reeling. Give us peace in all our questions and distress. Amen.

152. At the Birthday of an Aged Christian

Lord of love, we thank you for the _____ years of grace you have granted to your servant _____. We praise you for being with *him* in good days and evil, in joy and sorrow, in sickness and health. We praise you above all for having provided *him* with the rich comfort of your Word and sacraments. Continue to make these treasures *his* joy and delight. Be *his* strength, even when earthly strength fails. And finally bring *him* and all of us to the joy and glory of eternal life in your presence. Amen.

153. For Families

Almighty God, our heavenly Father, you set those who are lonely in families. We commend to your care all the homes in which your people live. Keep them free from bitterness, pride, and selfishness. Fill them with faith, wisdom, patience, and godliness. Let children and parents show respect for one another, and bless us all with a spirit of kindness and true affection. Amen.

154. For the Children of the Church

Heavenly Father, your Son embraced little children and welcomed them into his kingdom. We thank you for the joy of these little ones and implore you for calm strength and patient wisdom in caring for them. Send your holy angels to protect and defend them, and grant them grace to grow in the knowledge of your Word and to follow the example of our Savior Jesus Christ. Amen.

155. For Children—Without Christ

Lord Jesus, our Good Shepherd, hear our prayer for little ones. Look with compassion on all children who will enter their beds this night with no knowledge of your love to warm them, with no experience of your beauty to delight them, with no realization of your presence to comfort them. Send your holy angels to protect and defend them. Save them from suffering because of the sins of others, and bring them into the peace and safety of your kingdom. Amen.

156. For Youth

Lord God, heavenly Father, you see our young people growing up in an uncertain and confusing world. Send your Holy Spirit into their hearts so that they may grow in grace and wisdom. Give them strength to resist temptation and courage to meet the challenges of each new day. Show them that following you is more satisfying than pursuing selfish goals. Make their unique gifts and youthful vitality a blessing to their families, to the church, and to all others their lives may touch, through Jesus Christ, your Son, our Lord. Amen.

157. For Peace Between Siblings

Thank you, dear Father in heaven, for the brothers and sisters who have shared my home and my childhood. Thank you for their love and support over the years. When our sinful nature causes pain and strife between us, let the love of Jesus help us to forgive and to dry our tears. As you have made us one family on earth, grant that we may remain brothers and sisters in faith so that after we are separated by death, we may live forever with you in heaven. In Jesus' name we ask it. Amen.

158. Empty Nest

We thank you, dear Father in heaven, for the privilege of being parents. We thank you for all the times that our children have made us proud. And we ask forgiveness for every time we have failed to give our children what they need. Now that our children are grown, we pray that you would help us know when to step in and when to let go. Grant that our children and our grandchildren may continue to make us proud and follow in the faith that has guided us through the years so that we and our children may be reunited in heaven. Hear us for Jesus' sake. Amen.

159. For the Aged

Gracious heavenly Father, look with mercy on your servants who are facing new challenges and confronting change because of their increasing years. Grant them strength of body, peace of mind, and cheering companionship. Surround them with love and respect, concern and understanding. Enable them to accept assistance graciously and thankfully. As their time here on earth grows shorter, keep them strong in the faith, and assure them that you sustain them even to old age, through Christ our Lord. Amen.

160. When Someone Has Brought Disgrace on the Family

Lord Jesus, loving and compassionate Savior, we come to you with a burden that weighs heavily on our hearts. The conduct of our loved one has brought shame and disgrace within our family circle. Help us to bear this severe trial with humility and patience. Be merciful to _____. Show *him* the error of *his* ways and draw *him* back to you with the assurance of forgiveness, which you have earned for *him* by your innocent suffering and bitter death on the cross. By the power of your Holy Spirit, enable *him* in the future to stand firm in the hour of temptation and to walk in the way of your commandments, to the glory of your most holy name. Amen.

161. For a Child Who Doesn't Seem to Be Living His or Her Faith

Search my child, God. Know my child's heart. Test what is in my child's mind and all of *his* concerns and cares. See if there is any offensive way in *him,* and lead *him* in the way everlasting (Psalm 139:23,24). I am asking of my child what your Son asked of his disciples: "Where is your faith?" (Luke 8:25). Strengthen whatever faith remains in my child's heart. "Through the righteousness of our God and Savior Jesus Christ," grant my child "a faith as precious" as your Son granted his oft-doubting disciples (2 Peter 1:1). Amen.

162. When a Loved One Is Leaving Home

Dear heavenly Father, we pray for _____, who is leaving the security of *his* home. In *his* new and strange surroundings, comfort and sustain *him* with the assurance of your divine presence. Defend *him* against all danger; guard and protect *him* from all evil. Remind *him* often of your great love for *him* in Christ, so that by the power of the Holy Spirit, *he* may fear, love, and trust in you above all things. In the hour of perplexity and doubt, let your Word be a lamp to *his* feet and a light for *his* path. In the hour of trouble and fear, move *him* to turn to you in fervent and frequent prayer. Guide *him* in *his* search for true Christian friends who share *his* faith in Jesus and keep *him*, together with them and all of us, in the saving faith until we shall leave our earthly dwelling place to live with you in your eternal home. We ask through Jesus Christ our Lord. Amen.

163. To Not Take My Family for Granted

Heavenly Father, you have designed the exact times and places in which I live; you have placed me in my family to bless me. Keep me from taking my family for granted, and instead, show me regularly how truly valuable they are. Show me the sacrificial love of Christ, which made me a member of your eternal family, and give me the wisdom and ability to share that same love with my family. Watch over and care for all of our needs—both body and soul—so that we may one day experience perfect family life with you in heaven. Amen.

Prayers for Comfort

164. For Peace

O God of peace, I turn aside from an unquiet world, seeking rest for my spirit and light for my thoughts. I bring my work to be sanctified, my wounds to be healed, my sins to be forgiven, my hopes to be renewed. In you there is perfect harmony. Draw me to yourself, and silence the discords of my wasteful life. Your greatness is beyond my highest praise. Take me out of the loneliness of self, and fill me with the fullness of your peace. Amen.

165. A Personal Confession of Sin

Father, I have sinned against you and am no longer worthy to be called your child. Especially am I sorry for _____. Yet in mercy, you sacrificed your only Son to purge away my guilt. For his sake, O God, be merciful to me—a sinner—and in the joy of your Holy Spirit, let me serve you all my days. Amen.

166. For Forgiveness

Forgive us our sins, O Lord; forgive the sins of our past and the sins of our present, the sins of our souls and the sins of our bodies, our secret and our whispered sins, the sins we have done to please ourselves and the sins we have done to please others. Forgive our thoughtless and idle sins; forgive our serious and deliberate sins; forgive us those sins which we know and those sins which we do not know; forgive us the sins that we have labored so long to hide from others that we have hid them even from ourselves. Forgive them, O Lord; forgive them all. Through your great mercy absolve us of all our offenses; pardon and deliver us from all our iniquity. Cleanse us from all sin, through Jesus Christ our Lord. Amen.

167. Feeling Guilt

God of mercy, compassion, and healing, you are more willing to forgive than we are to confess. The burden of guilt is heavy upon us. We thank you that you hear us when we pray, that you share

our suffering and pain, and that you forgive our sins. Remind us
that with you, there is mercy, and let us hear joy and gladness.
Show us your mercy, O Lord, and grant us your salvation.
Through Jesus Christ our Lord. Amen.

168. Personal Disgrace

Gracious God, I thank you for having forgiven my sins and for
comforting me with this promise: "Though your sins are like
scarlet, they shall be as white as snow; though they are red as
crimson, they shall be like wool" (Isaiah 1:18). Strengthen my
faith, I implore you, and help me to live the rest of my days to
your glory so that the disgrace which I have brought on myself,
my church, and my loved ones may in due time be removed. Fill
the hearts of all who have been grievously offended by my sinful
conduct with a rich measure of your love so that they may be
merciful to me just as you have been merciful. Hear my prayer
through him who has made me acceptable in your sight, Jesus
Christ, my Redeemer. Amen.

169. For Faith That Whatever Sin My Pastor Forgives Is Forgiven in Heaven

Dear Savior, how I wish I could look you in the face and hear
you say, "I forgive you." I am so sorry for my sin, and I long for
your forgiveness. But you have given me the gift of a pastor, and
you have promised that whatever sins he forgives, you have
forgiven in heaven. Impress on me how real and valid these
words are. Strengthen my faith in that promise so that when he
tells me I am forgiven, it is just as if you were speaking to me, for
you speak through him. Amen.

170. For Patience

Lord Jesus, you promised to comfort those who mourn and to
satisfy those who hunger. In times of trial remind me of your
cross, where you endured the curse of my sin. When I am weak,
teach me to depend on you for strength. At your own time,
deliver me from suffering and distress. Amen.

171. For Obedience to God's Will

Lord God, give me strength and willingness to say with your Son, "Not my will, but yours be done" (Luke 22:42). Make me cheerful and trusting to bear whatever you let happen to me. From your hand I am willing to take the good and the bad, the joy and the sorrow. Keep me from sin, gracious Father, and comfort me with your kind Word. Amen.

172. For Help to Accept the Things I Cannot Change in Life

Heavenly Father, this is not how I want things to be. Remind me that it's not how you want things to be either. You want the perfection of heaven for all people. You want it so much that you sent your Son to die for the sins of the world. Christ wanted it so much that in the Garden of Gethsemane as he was facing something that he could not change, he prayed, "Not my will, but yours be done" (Luke 22:42). Forgive my lack of faith in you, for his sake. Keep his cross always before me so that I may never doubt your love for me. The one who died for me now lives again and knows how to lead me. Although I don't know the details, I know that your plan is perfect and leads all believers to heaven, so help me to pray with my Savior, "Not my will, but yours be done." Amen.

173. When God's Ways Are Hard to Understand

Gracious God, we turn to you in this hour of deep distress. We know that your thoughts are not our thoughts, neither are your ways our ways; for as the heavens are higher than the earth, so are your ways higher than our ways, and your thoughts than our thoughts (Isaiah 55:8,9). We do not ask to understand why _____ has happened to us, but we do implore you to comfort and sustain us with the assurance that your love in Christ will not fail in this hour. Strengthen us in the conviction that in all things, you work for the good of those who love you. Remove all doubts and complaints from our hearts, and help us in humble submission to say with Job, "The LORD gave and the LORD has taken away; may the name of the LORD be praised"

(1:21). We commit ourselves to your loving care now and forever, through Jesus Christ our Lord. Amen.

174. For Faith in God as Our Dear Father

Dear Father, earthly fathers discipline their children the best they can. But you are the only one who disciplines perfectly. Out of love for me, you show me my sin. Out of love for me, you sent your Son to be my Savior from sin. Help me trust you enough to endure hardship as discipline so that later on, it will produce a harvest of righteousness. Amen.

175. Remembering Loved Ones Who Died in the Lord

With reverence and affection we remember before you, O everlasting God, all our departed friends and relatives who died in Christ, especially _____. Keep us in union with them now through faith and love toward you so that after this life, we may enter into your presence and be numbered with those who serve you and look on your face in glory everlasting, through your Son, Jesus Christ our Lord. Amen.

176. Light for Today

What does it matter, O Lord, if the future is dark? I do not pray for tomorrow but for today. Keep my heart steadfast and grant me your light—just for today. Amen. (Theresa of Lisieux, 1873–1897)

177. For Courage

Lord Jesus, you have overcome the world and all power and authority is yours. When evil seems to triumph, give us courage and faith, and help us never to forget that you are with us everywhere, to the end of time. To you be glory now and forever. Amen.

178. Receiving News of a Death

O Father of mercies and God of all comfort, in this hour of sorrow we implore your grace to enable us to say in humble submission, "Your will be done." While our hearts are filled with sadness at the death of our loved one, our lips speak praise that you have removed *him* from all the trials and tribulations of this life and received *him* to yourself in heaven. Sustain us by the power of your Holy Word, which promises strength and help in time of need. Comfort us with the precious hope of the resurrection of the body and the life everlasting, through Jesus Christ our Lord. Amen.

Prayers for the Church and Christian Schools

179. For My Congregation

Dear Jesus, you state in your Word, "Where two or three gather in my name, there am I with them" (Matthew 18:20). I know that every time my congregation gathers for worship, you are there. I want to thank you, Lord, for this group of believers of which I am a part. Thank you for my pastor(s), teachers, and for those who serve our congregation in positions of authority. May their work be a blessing and not a burden. I also pray that all who hold membership may recommit themselves to be faithful in worship and that we might collectively use our time, talents, and treasures for your glory and our good. May your name be praised! Amen.

180. For Unity in My Congregation

Holy Spirit, Creator and sustainer of Christian unity, open my eyes to see the wonderful privilege it is to be intimately connected to the congregation into which you've brought me. Make the other members and me ever vigilant to the attacks of the devil's wicked schemes to sow the seeds of disunity and discord among us. By the power of your Word, defend us from those assaults of the evil one and strengthen the bonds of unity and peace in our congregation. Use me as an instrument of your peace in that effort. In the name of Jesus, the great reconciler. Amen.

181. For the Church

O triune God—Father, Son, and Holy Spirit—you have accomplished our salvation, creating us, redeeming us, and sanctifying us. Now we ask you to keep us in the fellowship of the saints and to bless your church everywhere. Grant that your Word may be taught in all its clarity and purity. Open hearts to receive it, and raise up more and more men, women, and children who know their Savior and worship you, the Father, the Son, and the Holy Spirit. Amen.

182. For Faithfulness to the Word

Merciful God, as you have said, "Let the one who has my word speak it faithfully" (Jeremiah 23:28), so lead all of our pastors, teachers, and professors to speak your Word faithfully in their ministries. Furthermore, lead all of our members to hear your Word regularly, to believe it wholeheartedly, to cling to it steadfastly, and to live by it daily. Amen.

183. For Sound Doctrine

Dear Holy Spirit, unless you keep us close to your Word, we will drift into false doctrine and error. Work on our hearts. Send us, if needed, trials and times of testing so that we are driven to study your Word for direction and comfort. Convince those who are not presently accepting clear and correct teaching. Guide those who are drifting away from the truth back to your Word. Above all, instill in everyone a love and appreciation for the gospel of your forgiveness. Amen.

184. For Pastors

Dear Lord of the harvest, give our pastors a love for the gospel of your forgiveness. When their ministry seems to spin off into many directions due to the many pressing problems they face in their congregations, bring them back to the gospel. Give them the confidence to put immediate concerns and problems lower on their priority list, if these matters are getting in the way of their ministering to people's eternal needs. Enable them truly to lift high your cross in every facet of their ministry and to spend themselves for the greatest cause on earth. Amen.

185. A Pastor's Prayer, When Feeling Burnt Out

O Father, Son, and Holy Spirit, your power to revive those who struggle is matchless. You have blessed me with the privilege of serving you as a pastor. But now I am struggling with doubts about whether I can continue to do this. So I fall before your throne, dear God, and seek your help. Use the power of your means of grace to renew my zeal for the pastoral ministry. Drive from me feelings of frustration and inadequacy. Lift me up, Lord, so that I can again be your instrument to lift others. Amen.

186. For When My Pastor Is Tempted

Son of God, Lord Jesus, Shepherd of God's flock, as you were tempted by Satan in the wilderness, so our pastor is assaulted by the enemy. Satan daily lays snares for our pastor—our shepherd—to bring shame upon him, to scandalize his ministry, and to render the Word of God ineffective. As you turned aside the devil's lies by the power of the Word, fill our pastor with your Spirit, surround him with your mighty angels, dress him in the full armor of God, and arm him with the sword of the Spirit so that he may ward off Satan's plot to scatter the flock. Keep him free of scandal and shame. Shield him also from false accusations. Help your people to keep him in prayer, to encourage him, and to avoid becoming a source of frustration and temptation for him. Let them build him up for his ministry. Grant that the good news of pardon and eternal life in Jesus flows unhindered from our church into our community. Amen.

187. For the Protection of My Pastor's Good Name

Lord Jesus, you are my Good Shepherd. In wisdom you have given me a pastor to shepherd my soul in this life. Grant that as he watches out for my soul, I may defend and protect his reputation. Help me to look at his words and actions in the kindest possible way. Make my ears a tomb where any gossip spoken about him immediately dies, and help me to correct any who speak ill of him. And if he should err, give me strength to speak to him with love and respect. Amen.

188. For All Pastors as They Prepare Their Sermons

Dear Father in heaven, as we sit at home on a Saturday night, we know that our pastor is meditating on the message he wants to share with us tomorrow. We pray that you would guide his thoughts. Help him understand the Scripture that he will share with us so that he will be able to apply it to our lives. Give him not only wisdom but also compassion so that he will comprehend our needs, comfort our souls, and encourage us in godly behavior in order for his preaching to bring honor to your name and peace to your people. In Jesus' name, we ask it. Amen.

189. For All Pastors—That Their Work Be a Joy, Not a Burden

Dear Jesus, my Savior, who served the world by giving your life as a ransom for all, thank you for calling men to be pastors—to be your servants who share your good news of forgiveness in your name. Let that privileged work bring joy to every pastor's heart, and keep them from getting burdened by other things—things like whether or not people "really listen" to their sermons, appreciate their work among them, or give them the respect they, in fact, deserve. Forgive all pastors for whenever they have looked too much at themselves and what they think they need, rather than looking at all you have done for them. Help them remember that they are immeasurably blessed to serve you by serving others with your Word and sacraments. In your name. Amen.

190. At a Church Anniversary

O God, you have promised to be with your church forever. We thank you for those who founded this community of believers and for the signs of your favor over these past years. Increase our faith, knit us together in the bonds of love, and make our fellowship an example to all people, through Jesus Christ our Lord. Amen.

191. At a Church Dedication

O almighty, everlasting God, you have joined together all believers into one spiritual temple in Christ. Look with favor on this church, which we have built to be a dwelling place for your glorious name and a house of prayer for your people. Accept it, O Lord, and bless our coming in and our going out from this time forth even forevermore, through Jesus Christ our Lord. Amen.

192. For the Synod

Lord Jesus, thank you for entrusting to me, through my synod, the preaching of your gospel in so many far-off places. Though even now the sun never sets on the work of my synod, nevertheless, use it further to witness your salvation to every nation on earth. Lest the gospel be hindered, watch over the synod's workers and their families everywhere, and supply their needs from the prayers and generous offerings of your people. Preserve scriptural unity and brotherly harmony in my synod, and equip its leaders for their high calling. Savior, I praise you. Amen.

193. For Laborers in God's Kingdom

Lord Jesus Christ, the sun is setting on the history of this world. You will soon return. Yet there are still so many who are lost in unbelief. Bless the church with an abundance of workers who are ready to enter your harvest fields. Give them zeal to reach the lost. Renew in them a sense of urgency. Lead us also to support them with our fervent prayers and generous offerings so that through them, your voice may be heard throughout the world. Glorify your name in all the earth, O Lord! Amen.

194. For Called Workers

Ascended Savior, hear our prayer for all whom you have called into the public ministry. Satisfy them with your rich and heavenly gifts. Cause your people to honor and respect them in their calling and to support them as those whom your Holy Spirit has made stewards of your Word and sacraments. Prosper their teaching and preaching of your Word among us so that we may grow in faith, wisdom, and good works. Amen.

195. For Worker Training

Lord of the harvest, give to your church men and women who are eager to prepare for service in your kingdom. Bless our schools with instructors who encourage and inspire their students to grow in grace and wisdom. Strengthen the resolve of students to complete their training for ministry, and send them out in the power of your Spirit. Amen.

196. For Newly Assigned Called Workers

Eternal Lord God, at the burning bush your servant Moses quaked with fear and reluctance when you called him into your service. Be with the young pastors and teachers who are going out into your harvest field for the first time. Calm their nervousness with the assurance that they go in your name. Dismiss their doubts by reminding them that the power behind their ministry lies in your Word and not in their persons. Fill them with joy for the privilege of being your representatives, and keep them faithful by reminding them that they are not working for men but for you, our faithful God. Bless their work to your great glory. Amen.

197. For Synodical Officials and Leaders

Lord of the church, in whose name our synodical officials and leaders who oversee and serve your flock have been called, grant them all the gifts necessary for the godly administration of their duties, the upbuilding of your church, and the glory of your name; for you live and reign with the Father and the Holy Spirit, one God, now and forever. Amen.

198. For Lay Leaders in the Church

Lord Jesus, we thank you for giving lay leaders in your church a variety of useful gifts for serving your people in the faith. Send your Holy Spirit to encourage and direct them in their work for the common good of all believers and the glory of your name. Amen.

199. The School Year

"Start children off on the way they should go, and even when they are old they will not turn from it" (Proverbs 22:6). The start of another school year reminds us of this exhortation from you, Lord. Help us to realize the importance of the education and the training of children. We ask you to bless all those who labor in the schools around our nation. We ask you to bless both our Christian schools and the public schools. Prosper also the educational efforts of parents and congregations and grant that the rising generation may not only grow in secular wisdom but also grow in knowledge of you, the only true God, and your Son Jesus Christ, in whose name we pray. Amen.

200. Christian Education

Lord Jesus, teacher of the truth, keep the light of Christian education glowing in your church. Enter our Christian elementary schools and Sunday schools. With your powerful Word, mold the intellect, will, values, and habits of our children. Give your gospel success at our Lutheran high schools to keep our teenagers on the narrow road. Watch closely over our synod's preparatory schools, colleges, and theological seminary so that your flock may be provided with faithful pastors and teachers. We seek these blessings in the hope that our children and our children's children may learn to know your name. Amen.

201. For the Schools of the Church

Lord Jesus, ascended Savior, you have commanded us to instruct the young in your saving truth. Bless the schools of our church and all other agencies through which we work together to carry out that vital task. Give wisdom to those who teach and attentive ears and eager hearts to those who learn. Grant that your Word may be passed down from one generation to the next, until all your lambs are safely gathered into your eternal fold. Amen.

202. For Teachers in Christian Schools

Dear Lord Jesus, you commanded your disciples to let the children come to you. You blessed them and reminded us that your kingdom belongs to such as these. Many in our synod have the privilege of bringing their children to teachers you have prepared. Bless the work of our teachers during this school year. May the precious message of the gospel be their dearest treasure, a treasure they delight to teach our children. And for the sake of your gospel, give our teachers strength, patience, understanding, and wisdom as they teach the knowledge and skills our children will need in the future. Amen.

203. For Adult Spiritual Education

Lord Jesus, it is your will that believers continue to grow in grace and knowledge throughout their lives. Fill the members of our congregation with a deep love for your Word and a desire to hear and learn it. Use our Bible classes, together with all other opportunities our congregation offers to study the Scriptures, as workshops of your Spirit. Nourish and strengthen the faith of many, so that we may grow together toward spiritual maturity. Hear us for your mercy's sake. Amen.

204. For the Erring

Merciful and gracious God and Father, we earnestly implore you to turn the hearts of all who have forsaken the faith they once embraced, who have wandered from it, or who are in doubt about your truth. Mercifully touch their hearts and restore them so that they may wholeheartedly take pleasure in your Word, which alone can make them wise for salvation through faith in Jesus Christ, our Lord. Amen.

205. For Those Straying From the Church

Gentle Shepherd, you have warned me that the devil prowls around like a roaring lion, seeking someone to devour. And you have told me that you will not snuff out the smoldering wick. Preserve the faith of those who wander away from hearing your Word and tasting your Holy Supper. Give them repentance to see the urgency of returning to your church. Give me the opportunity of sharing your truth with them. Amen.

206. Missions

Lord, there is urgency and ecstasy in proclaiming the message of your great love. Allow your Word to have free course so that it may be declared among all peoples of the world. May I cheerfully support the cause of the gospel. Bless those who labor in far-off lands, away from loved ones and familiar places. Keep our missionary families healthy and in love with you as well as with one another. May their courage and zeal for the gospel be an example to us whenever we feel tired or are tempted to be

apathetic, and may they always be found eager and willing to
serve you and your holy name. Amen.

207. Missionaries

Dear God, we recognize your command to go into all the world
and preach the gospel to every creature. Many of us cannot be
directly active in carrying out this commission. Therefore, we
have sent missionaries in our name around the world to preach
your Word. We come to you on behalf of those missionaries. Be
with them, and help them feel your love. Keep them safe from all
dangers. Keep them faithful to their task, and bless their efforts
to bring others to know their Savior. Amen.

208. For Christians in Other Lands

Lord God, in your mercy you have blessed our land with
freedom to worship you without threat and with ease. We
pray for your people who live in places where this is not the
case, where Christians face peril daily for their faith or where
ministry to your people is difficult. Be with them, dear Lord,
and strengthen them to endure their suffering. It is sad to
think about that suffering, but it is joyful to think about how,
at every hour, someplace in the world, there are saints awake
praising you: "Where morning dawns, where evening fades,
you call forth songs of joy" (Psalm 65:8). No hatred or peril
can stop those songs. Keep all Christians everywhere safe until
you grant us rest in the glory of heaven. In our Savior's name,
we pray. Amen.

209. For Persecuted Christians

Almighty Lord Jesus, just as the world once considered you
worthy of abuse and violence, so many who follow you
are treated the same today. Be with those who are actively
persecuted for their faith. Show them that in you, they have
a companion who has experienced unjust pain and suffering;
they have a companion who has triumphed over every evil
and now shares that victory with them, even in times of trial
and weakness. Provide for them the patient endurance that

will lead them through every trial to a life of eternal glory with you. Amen.

210. For Special Ministries

Lord of life and love, we ask your blessings on our ministries to those with special needs. When you walked this earth, you showed tender compassion to all. You turned no one away. Help us reflect your gentle compassion as we strive to serve those with special needs. Give us the wisdom, ability, patience, and resources to effectively communicate the good news of Jesus to all, regardless of their circumstances. Encourage us with your promises that whatever we do for others, we do for you. And bring us at last to the sinless perfection of our eternal home with you. Amen.

211. At a Church Worker's Retirement

Eternal God, we give you thanks for your servant _____ and for *his* ministry in your church. Give *him* the grace to remain faithful in your service now and evermore, and grant that those deeds begun in your name may, by the power of your Holy Spirit, grow and flourish, through Jesus Christ our Lord. Amen.

212. At the Death of a Congregation's Pastor

O Lord Jesus, head of the church and chief Shepherd of your flock, it has pleased you to call the pastor of this congregation from this earthly life to heavenly glory. While we mourn his death, we rejoice in the eternal victory he now shares with you. We thank you for the blessings you bestowed on your servant, Pastor _____ , for bringing him to faith, for preserving him in faith, and for giving him the joy of publicly proclaiming your Word and administering your sacraments. You have kept him faithful to your Word and made him a blessing to us and to many others. Grant a special measure of comfort to his family as they mourn his loss, and give healing to their sorrowing hearts through the precious assurances of your Word. May the death of our pastor remind us all of the frailty of life, and may your Holy

Spirit ever keep before us the goal of everlasting life. Hear us and comfort us for Jesus' sake. Amen.

213. At the Death of a Congregation's Teacher

Almighty God, eternal fountain of all wisdom, it has pleased you to call to his heavenly home the soul of this teacher of the lambs of your flock. We thank you for having made _____ your child and for having given *him* the grace to devote *his* life and talents to the training and instruction of the young. We praise you for having blessed *his* efforts to plant the precious seed of your Word in the hearts of our children and for *his* example of humility, patience, and unselfish Christian love. Look with compassion on those bowed down by the death of your servant, and sustain them with the comfort of your gospel. Be for them a very present help in trouble. Direct our thoughts heavenward so that we may ever seek the one thing needful, the knowledge of our Lord and Savior Jesus Christ, who conquered death so that we may live with you forever. Amen.

214. For Baptism Sponsors

Thank you, Jesus, for the saving power of Baptism. I thank you also for those people who are willing to be sponsors. Remind them of what a special privilege it is to love and pray for their godchild. Remind them of what a solemn obligation it is to do all they can to keep their godchild close to you. Equip them with devotion and love for the task. If or when I am chosen to be a sponsor, fill me with such love for that child and for you that I may be faithful to the vows I make. Amen.

215. For Young People Preparing for Confirmation

Lord God, heavenly Father, in Holy Baptism you began your good work in these young believers. You have also blessed their training and instruction in your Word, so that they now look forward to their confirmation and to receiving your Holy Communion. We pray that you would pour out your Holy Spirit on their hearts and minds as they study your Word so they may truly love and fear you, confess their faith joyfully and boldly, and with their lips and their lives glorify you, their faithful God and Lord, through Jesus Christ, their Savior and ours. Amen.

216. After a Call Has Been Extended

Lord Jesus, you instituted the office of the public ministry and have given your people the privilege of extending calls to serve us through that ministry. Having asked for your help and guidance, our congregation has called _____ to serve us as _____. We ask that as *he* prayerfully considers this call, you would guide *him* to a decision that is in the best interest of your kingdom. As we await *his* decision, bless our congregation and its ministry so that your kingdom may continue to grow and flourish among us. We ask this in your name, for you are the Good Shepherd and head of the church. Amen.

217. After a Call Has Been Accepted

Lord of the church, we thank you for answering our prayers by leading _____ to accept our call to serve as _____. We pray that you would grant *him* the wisdom to use faithfully the gifts you have given *him* to fulfill *his* ministry among us. Help us honor and respect *him* as your gift to our congregation. Enable us to work together with *him* and all our called workers in a spirit of harmony and love so that your kingdom may flourish among us and come also to the hearts of others, to the glory of your holy name. Amen.

Prayers for the Nation and Society

218. Agriculture

Heavenly Father, you keep your promises that seedtime and harvest will always continue. We ask that there be enough to feed your creation. To that end, bless the efforts of those who sow and reap, who tend the cattle and work the soil. Make favorable the conditions of growth and bless the increase. Let us, together with all people, recognize your gracious blessings. Those who are hungry, Lord, sustain. Move the hearts of those with an abundance to share with those who have not. Relieve hunger and the suffering that accompanies it. In mercy, Lord, hear our prayer. Amen.

219. For Healthy Livestock

Lord of all, every animal we own truly belongs to you. Livestock are your gracious gift, intended to benefit us and our society. Yet in this sinful world sickness, hardship, accidents, suffering, and death afflict not only us but also the animals entrusted to our care. Bless our livestock with safety, good health, and proper care so that we and many others will be blessed through them. Relieve our anxiety that comes from taking care of them with the reminder that you are the One who provides for us and all things. Grant us wisdom to care for them to the best of our knowledge, resources, and ability and to the glory of your name. Amen.

220. For the Harvest

King of creation, we ask your blessing upon the harvest of our land. Protect us from those natural disasters that may reduce the effectiveness of our labors. Grant us a bountiful harvest, and give us grace to receive this bounty with thankful hearts. Let us use the fruits of the earth in true wisdom, without selfishness, and to your glory. Grant that this harvest may meet not only our needs but also the needs of all your creatures. Finally, fill our hearts with that gratitude which moves us to share freely with others what we have received from your generosity. In Jesus' name. Amen.

221. For the Environment

Almighty God, in giving us dominion over things on earth, you made us fellow workers in this world you have created. Give us wisdom and reverence to use the resources of nature so that no one may suffer from our abuse of them and generations yet to come may continue to praise you for your bounty; through your Son, Jesus Christ our Lord. Amen.

222. For Our Country

Dear heavenly Father, thank you for the many years of blessings that you have showered upon our land. Thank you for your gift of prosperity in days of peace and protection in days of war. Thank you for our natural resources, our talents, and our abilities. Thank you for giving us freedom of worship and all the other freedoms we possess. We confess that we are sinners and deserve nothing. Nevertheless, for Jesus' sake, we ask you to accompany us with your forgiving grace. Bless our government, prosper the work of our hands, and especially enable us to fulfill our responsibilities as citizens of your kingdom of grace and to be conscientious citizens of this good land. Amen.

223. The Unborn

Merciful God almighty, King Herod once murdered infants in an effort to kill your Son. For many years now our own government has allowed the slaughter of millions more infants in defiance of your Son. Our cry goes up, "O Lord, how long?" We pray, dear God, give wisdom to our rulers to outlaw these killings once again. Give grace to the unborn to keep them in your care now and for eternity. Give understanding to mothers to nurture and provide for their babies. And grant forgiveness to all of us who actively or passively have been a part of this great national sin. We beg you, in Jesus' name. Amen.

224. Peace Among Nations

Lord and Maker of all people, impress on people of every nation that they are the children of your creation. Lord and ruler of nations, bless all efforts to promote peace and understanding among the nations of the world. Lord and Savior of the world, remove hatred and enmity from the hearts of people. Enable people everywhere to live at peace with one another. Direct all leaders of government to strive for peace and to conduct international relations so that more people may live in quietness and peace. We pray this in the name of the Prince of peace. Amen.

225. In Time of National Calamity

Sovereign Lord, we bow low before you in this time of national calamity. We confess that as a nation, we have deserved your chastening judgments. Yet we also trust your promises that, even when you chasten, your purposes are loving and good. Be present with your strong comfort among those most directly affected by this calamity, and in your mercy make shattered lives whole again. Use this tragedy to make us as a nation deeply aware of our total dependence on you. Give us courage to face whatever the future holds, knowing that it—and we—are in your hands. Amen.

226. In Times of National Conflict

You, O Lord, occupy the highest heavens. Look down in mercy on this our nation. Turn the hearts of our enemies to peace. Guard and protect us from the efforts of those who seek to terrorize and destroy us, and stop those who use your name to excuse their evil. Continue to bless our land with the freedoms that have enabled us to worship you openly. Give us wise rulers who will govern with justice and equity and concern for the people under their rule. Finally, keep us in faith so that, whether in life or in death, we will be yours. Amen.

227. After Natural Disasters

Almighty God, merciful Father, our ever-present help in time of trouble, once again we have come to realize that your thoughts are not our thoughts, your ways are not our ways. In your wisdom you have permitted a disastrous *fire, flood, earthquake* to cause pain and loss. Do not let the hearts of your people despair, but sustain and comfort them. Heal the injured, console the bereaved and afflicted, protect the helpless, and deliver all who are still in danger, through Jesus Christ our Lord. Amen.

228. In Times of Drought and Famine

Merciful God and Father, Lord of all creation, we are weary and discouraged because of the drought that has settled on our land. We implore you to remember our need for rain to revive and refresh the earth. Do not let our crops wither and die for lack of moisture, but open the heavens and send gentle, plentiful rain. The conditions that threaten us make us realize that we can plant and cultivate, but you alone can bring growth and produce a harvest. Graciously hear our prayer. Amen.

229. Thanksgiving for Rain

Most gracious God and Father, we thank and praise you for once again sending rain to water the parched earth, causing it to be fruitful and to bring forth food for humans and animals. Help us always to remember that, without your blessing, crops cannot grow and food cannot nourish. Continue to bless us with rainfall and sunshine in proper measure so that seedtime and harvest may preserve us for your service. Make us truly grateful for all the blessings you provide each day as our loving Creator. Amen.

230. For Social Justice

O Lord, you work righteousness and justice for all who are oppressed. Move the hearts of all people so that the barriers that unjustly divide us may crumble, suspicions may disappear, and hatred may cease. Heal our divisions so that we might live in peace, through your Son, Jesus Christ our Lord. Amen.

231. In Times of Civil Unrest

Heavenly Father, Lord of the nations, look in mercy on our nation as we struggle with discord and civil unrest. Frustrate the plans of those who would stir up violence and strife, and bless the efforts of all who promote harmony and peace. Give to our leaders and all in authority a special measure of wisdom and patience as they carry out their tasks, and grant that justice may prevail throughout our land. Help us as Christian citizens to reflect your love in all we do. Let the preaching of your gospel, which alone can bring true peace to human hearts, be heard throughout our land. Hear us for the sake of Jesus, the Prince of peace, our Savior. Amen.

232. For Police Officers

Triune God, I pray to you on behalf of the police officers of our land. Protect those who protect us. As ones who see the sinfulness and ugliness of our fallen world in ways that I do not, guide the officers to see that the role they fill is good. Lead them away from the temptation to have a cold and calloused heart. And above all, as ones who may be called on to lay down their lives for others, through your Word let them see the Savior who first laid down his life for them. Amen.

233. In Times of War

O Lord, ruler of nations and Savior of all people, we pray that you would look with mercy on our world now engaged in war and bring this conflict to a rapid end. We bow to your will and hold fast to your promise that you are ruling the world for the welfare of those who love you. We remember before you today the men and women who serve in our nation's armed forces. Be with them, protect them, and help them faithfully to carry out their difficult duties. Relieve the anxious thoughts of loved ones who are concerned about the safety of our armed forces. We know, Lord, that the ultimate cause of war is sin. Lead us to repent of our sins and hold fast to your forgiving love. When you determine to restore peace, grant that what is just and right in your eyes will prevail. We ask this for Jesus' sake. Amen.

234. For Those in the Armed Forces

Heavenly Father, bless our fellow citizens who are serving in our country's armed forces. Keep them ever in your love and protection. Give whatever help is needed to carry out their duties. Be with them in their lonely hours. Keep them from sin.

Protect them in the discharge of their many assignments, and bring them safely again to their homes and families. Amen.

235. For Our Enemies

O God, Lord of all, your Son commanded us to love all—even our enemies—and to pray for them. Deliver us from prejudice, hatred, and cruelty. Help us endure unjust treatment without seeking revenge. Fill our hearts with the forgiving love that we learn only from Christ. And may that love so move the hearts of our enemies so that one day they and we may stand before you, reconciled to you and to one another, through your Son, Jesus Christ our Lord. Amen.

236. For Peace

Lord Jesus, you are the Prince of peace. By your life, death, and resurrection, you earned for us peace with God. In a restless and turbulent world, enable us who know your peace to be peacemakers. Help us by word and example to promote harmony in our homes, workplaces, churches, schools, and wherever you place us in life. Amen.

237. Thanksgiving for Peace Restored

Gracious God and Father, you have put an end to the destruction and horrors of war. We thank you for your mercy and for having heard our humble requests. Heal the wounds this war has inflicted, and build up again what has been laid waste. Preserve the peace that you have restored, and remove hatred and ill will between nations. May peaceful conditions in our world provide the opportunity for your church to proclaim the good news of salvation everywhere so that your peace—a peace far greater than earthly peace—may come to human hearts, through Jesus Christ, the Savior of all. Amen.

238. Before an Election

Lord God, Lord of nations, you have made us citizens both of your kingdom of grace and of the earthly nation in which we live. You have placed us under a government that gives us the privilege of choosing the leaders who govern us. As another election approaches, help us appreciate and use this privilege. Bless our nation through the election of honest and responsible officials, and watch over us each day with your almighty protection and your unfailing love. Amen.

239. After an Election

Lord and ruler of nations, you tell us not to trust in mortal princes but to place our faith in you. By your most holy and powerful Word, strengthen our resolve to do that more and more. Help us to be mindful, as your children, of your desire that we pay proper respect and honor to our nation's newly elected officials because they draw their authority from you. Guide them with your eternal wisdom, and use them for your holy purposes. In the name of Jesus, King of kings and Lord of lords, amen.

240. For Civil Authorities

Lord God, ruler of all, we commend our nation and its leaders to your care. Bless our *president*, the members of *Congress*, and all officials who serve us in *state*, *county*, and local governments. Impress on all who are in authority the sacredness of the responsibility you have placed on them. Give them the gifts required for leadership, wisdom to make laws that will bring order and justice to our society, and compassion for the downtrodden and the poor. Purge our land from dishonesty and corruption in government. Teach us to honor all civil authorities as your representatives. Through stable government provide throughout our land an atmosphere in which your church can do its work in peace. Amen.

241. For an Honest Government

Almighty God, the governing authorities have been established by you to maintain good order in society. Yet those in government often lie and deceive to achieve their own purposes, and our nation and its people suffer. Grant us honest leaders who seek not their own interests but the welfare of those they serve. Then order will be maintained, our nation will benefit, and your kingdom within this great nation of ours will prosper and grow. I ask this in Jesus' name. Amen.

242. For Communities

Lord God, you have graciously given us the companionship of friends and neighbors by placing us in communities where we may live in harmony and work together for the good of society. Keep us free from selfishness, indifference, and prejudice. Lead us to seek the welfare of others, and make us willing to contribute to the improvement of our neighborhoods, towns, and cities so that people of diverse cultures and differing talents may enjoy peace, justice, and good order, through Christ our Lord. Amen.

243. For Natural Resources

Lord God, you put Adam and Eve in the Garden of Eden to work it and care for it, surrounded by its beauty. Increase in us the love you want us to have for your creation. Give us wisdom to use the abundant resources of nature with discretion and prudence. Teach us to honor you by our careful regard for the work of your hands. Enable us to use and enjoy your bounty responsibly so that generations yet to come may delight in the richness of your creation. Amen.

244. For Proper Use of Wealth

Lord God, our Creator and preserver, your blessings are "new every morning; great is your faithfulness" (Lamentations 3:23). You have given us material wealth far more than we require for our basic needs. Preserve us from apathy, complacency, and selfishness. Keep us from so avidly pursuing prosperity that in gaining the world, we lose our souls. Lead us to use wisely and for your glory the things you have entrusted to our care. Make us always grateful for your generosity, and move us to share generously with others. Hear us for Jesus' sake. Amen.

Prayers for God's Blessing Upon Various Professions and Callings

245. For Those Entering College

Lord Jesus, I pray for all those who are beginning their college education. Help all of them to daily appreciate what a privilege and opportunity it is, as well as the wealth of knowledge that is now before them. Grant them diligence, discernment, and discipline as they study. I pray especially that you calm their fears and doubts and lead them to make good, godly decisions every day and every night. Please let their higher education expose them most of all to the heights of your Word so that they learn your will and never depart from it—so that they grow not just in worldly knowledge but in wisdom and faith, walking with you through college halls and beyond. Amen.

246. For Graduates

O Holy Spirit, sent by Jesus to guide us into all truth, shower your gifts and graces on all graduates. Make them truly grateful to all who have helped them with their education. Enable them to use the lessons they have learned to advance their own welfare, to serve others, and to glorify your name. As they step into an uncertain future, strengthen them through your Word and sacraments so that they may be comforted and reassured by your presence. Teach them to demonstrate true wisdom and understanding by fearing and loving you and by keeping your commandments. We pray in Jesus' name, who, with you and the Father, are one Lord now and forever. Amen.

247. For Child Care Providers, Teachers, and School Staff

Dear God, you remind us that "children are a heritage from the LORD, offspring a reward from him" (Psalm 127:3). Instill in child care workers, teachers, and school staffers a love of your Word to equip them with the desire to treat children as the gifts they are from you. Give child educators commitment and dedication to their work of assisting parents to raise children who glorify your name. May educators and parents unite in efforts to keep children in your grace as they mature in education and faith into adulthood. There is such great joy when children know you as Lord and continue to teach the next generation all about you, our Father, Son, and Holy Spirit, overflowing in grace. Amen.

248. For Doctors, Health Care, and Public Health Workers

Thank you, Lord, for giving us doctors, nurses, and all those in the health care field. They have the unique challenge of holding our physical lives in their hands. I pray that you would bless their training, their skills, and their decisions for the health and well-being of their patients. When they become discouraged, lift them up. Keep them dedicated to their work of healing people. Teach them to rely on you, and remind them that they can do nothing without you. Amen.

249. For Factory Workers, Builders, Miners, and Craftspeople

Almighty Father, by your mighty hand you crafted and built this world and everything in it. In your wisdom you have gifted my neighbors with skills to use the natural resources you have created for their own crafting and building. Help them do so to your glory and for the benefit of their fellow human beings in this life. Help them to work diligently, not only for the sake of those who will use what they make but also so that they may provide for their families and have income to use to help those in need. Amen.

250. For Home Caregivers

Heavenly Father, we thank you for the many who provide care for the ill and troubled among us. Give to all caregivers sympathy and compassion as they comfort, encourage, and help those whom they support. Keep them from becoming weary in well-doing, and give them strength to continue to reach out to those in need. As they come to know better the love of Christ, move them to love others and so imitate our Savior in his untiring service and self-sacrifice. In his name we pray. Amen.

251. For Musicians and Artists

God, our Creator, we thank you for giving joy and delight to your church through those who are skilled in music and the arts. Lead them to develop more and more the gifts you have given them, to dedicate their talents to your worship, and to serve your people in humility. Make us grateful for their efforts, and move us to encourage and support them. Use them to bring echoes and reflections of your beauty to the ears and eyes of many so that, having experienced your beauty, they may also seek your goodness and truth to the glory of Christ our Lord. Amen.

252. For Office Workers

Lord, watch over all office workers. Help them not to feel like a mere cog in the corporate machine. So much of the work they do may seem to go unnoticed and unappreciated. They see the "suits" walk by, oblivious to the many at their desks, in their cubicles, and at their workbenches—the "nameless," "faceless" people who really keep the businesses running. First, I pray, lead the workers to be thankful for work that uses their skills and pays their bills. Let that be fulfilling to them! Then, open their eyes to see the opportunities to encourage their coworkers, especially with your Word, when they are having a bad day. Show them that this is their private ministry. Finally, I pray, keep the administrators aware that company success comes from the skills and labor of the workers you have provided for them. Move them to treat their workers fairly. Let every office worker go home each day in the satisfaction of knowing that, in serving others, they have served you. Amen.

253. For Relief Workers in Perilous Lands

Dear Heavenly Father, we thank you for those brave souls who have put their lives at risk in order to bring relief to people in places that are torn by strife and disease. We ask you to bless their labors so that they may have the joy of success and the appreciation of the people they serve. Protect them from those who would cause them harm. And when they suffer loss or injury, give them the courage to continue to serve to the honor of your name and the welfare of their neighbors. In Jesus' name, we ask it. Amen.

254. For Researchers and Scientists

Dear Father in heaven, we thank you for those talented people who have dedicated their lives to the discovery of those mysteries which you have hidden in nature. We ask you to grant success to the long hours spent in research. When they are frustrated in their efforts to find some new cure, give them patience to try again in their efforts to relieve weakness and pain. When they are tempted to pursue activities that would contradict your will, help them to see the danger and to follow your guidance so that their labors do not add to human suffering. In Jesus' name we ask it. Amen.

255. For Those Who Clean Up After the Rest of Us

We thank you, dear Father in heaven, for the unseen people who clean up the messes we leave behind. In our home we see the mess and clean it up eventually. But in public places we are not so careful to be neat. Thank you for those who come in after we leave to make the place neat again. And that includes those who clean up after our careless or sinful behavior. Grant success to their efforts so that we may not create problems in the lives of others. In Jesus' name we pray. Amen.

256. For Those Who Maintain Our Communications and Power Grids

Lord God, you make the clouds your chariot and the winds your messengers (Psalm 104:3,4). Thank you for giving mere humans the intelligence and ingenuity to overcome our communication barriers through your gifts of light and energy. Thank you for the gifts of infrastructure that allow us the luxuries of lights, televisions, and phones. Bless the men and women who harness electricity and radio frequencies through the design and construction of communications and power grids. Keep safe those who scale the heights and excavate the depths in service to grid maintenance. Lift their eyes toward you, and let their humble service be their own personal act of worship. Through Christ our Lord. Amen.

257. For Those Who Provide Food, Shelter, and Grooming

Lord God, you open your hand and satisfy my desires. Though you could provide for all my needs directly, more often you do so through the helping hands of others. You bless me through all who faithfully serve in vocations that bring food to my table to nourish me. Thank you for all whose work assists in building, providing, and maintaining our homes: I'm grateful. For all who work to provide goods and services that assist me in caring for the body you've given me, I give you thanks! Prosper the work of these people's hands. Amen.

258. For Those Who Work in Finance and Real Estate

Heavenly Father, you created the material world in which we live. Forgive me whenever I value it more than I do you and your kingdom of grace. Thank you for those who work in finance and real estate to help others enjoy the benefits of wealth and property. Lead them to always serve their clients in ways that have their neighbors' best interests in mind and not their own. Keep all of us focused on storing up treasures in heaven, as our Lord Jesus teaches us to do. Amen.

259. For Those Who Work in Retail

Every item in every shopping cart and shopping bag comes from you, Lord. You use merchants and store workers to get good food and clothing to us. Thank you. Bless and protect those who work in stores or markets. Keep them from being taken advantage of (Deuteronomy 24:14). Protect them against any temptation to deal dishonestly with their customers (25:16). Let their break room conversations be a blessing to one another. Lead them to trust you amid whatever stresses arise and to persistently bring cheerful encouragement to everyone who shops in their store. Amen.

260. For Those Who Work in the Media

Storytellers, playactors, singers, and messengers have always had a lot of power over the human heart—and now, through satellite signals and fiber-optic networks, that power crosses many miles and touches millions. God of every heart, give a spirit of wisdom to those who work in the media. Help them be as careful with their messages as your holy Levites watching over your Word (Deuteronomy 33:9) or even as the Israelites marching around Jericho, whom Joshua commanded, "Do not say a word until the day I tell you" (Joshua 6:10). Keep them from leading anyone, especially our young people, into sin. Make them a blessing to families and society. Amen.

261. For Truck Drivers and Pilots

Dear Lord, God of all travelers, you led Abraham throughout Canaan and brought Israel's millions through the Red Sea and the flooding Jordan (Joshua 24:3,7,11). Safely lead all who steer through land, sea, and air through the daylight and the night. Watch over them, their cargo, their passengers, and all who might cross their paths. Keep them prayerful during the long hours. Keep them faithful to their families during their time away from home. Guard them against drowsiness, equipment failure, and all who would do them harm. Protector of Israel, protect them on their entire journey and among all the nations through which they travel (24:17). Amen.

Prayers for Spiritual Gifts

262. For a Repentant Heart

Lord God, heavenly Father, I have offended you. I try to hide my sin, yet your eyes see. I try to laugh away my guilt, but I know that my guilt is eternally serious. My sin stokes your righteous anger. My rebellion causes your heart pain. Help me see my sin, feel the separation from you that it causes, and repent of it. Lift up my heart to you with the forgiveness and peace that I so desperately need. Lord, you came to save sinners, of whom I am the worst (1 Timothy 1:15). Amen.

263. For Godly Sorrow Over My Sins

Holy Father, too often I think of sin as a good thing. I think that I will find pleasure in sin and that I can solve my problems by sinning. My real problem is that I don't trust you. You are loving. If you call something a sin, I should trust that it is evil. Wondrously, you not only still love me but sent your Son to die for my sins, knowing already all the evil I would do. Forgive me for his sake. Help me to fear, love, and trust in you above all things so that I can see my sins for the abomination that they really are. Lead me to godly sorrow so that I turn from my evil ways. Comfort me with your gospel so that I live for you. Move me to follow your commands because you are the light of the world. Amen.

264. For a Mind Open to Scripture

Almighty, everlasting God, Lord, heavenly Father, whose Word is a lamp to my feet and a light for my path, open and enlighten my mind so that I may understand your Word purely, clearly, and devoutly, and then, having understood it correctly, pattern my life according to it, in order that I may never displease you; through Jesus Christ, your Son, our dear Lord. Amen. (John Bugenhagen, 1485–1558)

265. For Taking Scripture to Heart

Blessed Lord, you have given us your Holy Scriptures for our learning. May we so hear them, read, learn, and take them to heart that, being strengthened and comforted by your Holy Word, we may cling to the blessed hope of everlasting life, through Jesus Christ our Lord. Amen.

266. For Increased Appreciation for the Old Testament

Lord God, Holy Spirit, giver of God's Word, I love the Bible for its message of pardon for sin and of eternal life in Jesus. I love the New Testament for its engaging stories and for its clear teachings of Jesus and the apostles. I have to admit that the Old Testament is "flyover country" for me; I'm frustrated by it and just don't feel a great need to read it. Okay, I know this is wrong, so I must ask you, Holy Spirit, for your help with my attitude. You are the author of the entire Bible. It is your tool for bringing people to faith and for changing lives. Open my mind and heart to see Jesus throughout the Bible—to see the Old Testament fulfilled in the New and the New Testament built on the Old. Help me to realize that people who lived before Jesus' time on earth had God's entire plan of salvation in Jesus laid out before them in Old Testament prophecy. Give me teachers who are firmly grounded in the entirety of Scripture to lead me in my studies. Come, Holy Spirit, to enlighten me, for you are the author of all of God's Word. Amen.

267. For Renewed Wonder at the Miracles of Christ

Dear all-powerful Lord, how often and shamefully I yawn at the mention of the miracles you performed during your earthly ministry. Convict my heart of this wrong, and daily comfort me with your Word of forgiveness for this and every sin. Renew the wonder in my heart to think of your power, which you used always in mercy. Make me marvel even more that you laid aside this power to carry out the work of salvation on Calvary's cross. Comfort me to know that you are always my all-powerful, all-wise, and all gracious Savior. In your saving name I pray. Amen.

268. For Delight in God's Word: Both His Laws and His Promises

Lord, you inspired the psalmist to write, "Your word is a lamp for my feet, a light on my path" (Psalm 119:105). If only it were more of a delight than it is for me to have the gift of your Word. It is so true, so profound, so enlightening, but I take it so for granted. As I study your Word, may it be as if I hear you in my room talking to me. May I find you revealing your will for me in the law, which shows me my sin and convinces me there is no way to live outside your law. Show me that I need your help to live as I should. Then with your gospel lead me to see my deliverance from sin and obtain the righteousness only Jesus gives. As long as I live, may I never cease to be thrilled by your life-giving Word. Amen.

269. For the Fear of God

You shake the earth, you quake the mountains, the stars fight for you, and the rivers sweep away your foes (Judges 5:4,5,20,21), but my heart trembles so little before you. I join in the careless attitudes and proud postures that your enemies take in their rebellion against you. Set me to trembling at your greatness. Impress upon my heart the seriousness of your anger toward sin. Make clear to me what's at stake in my every waking minute, in every temptation, in every distraction that would cause me to forget about your glory. Fill me with respect, awe, and childlike fear of you, God of all holiness. Amen.

270. For God's Love

God our Father, your Son welcomed all who came to him, even the outcasts and despised. Give me a faith that dares to come to you, trusting only in your love. Give me a love that accepts others, as I have been accepted by you. Amen.

271. For Love of Others

Lord Jesus, teach me to love others as you have loved me. Help me be more patient and alert to the needs of others and always ready to serve them with the gifts you have given me. Amen.

272. For a Heart That Loves the Unlovable

Dear Lord Jesus, in this sinful world there are people who are hard to love, sometimes myself included. Arrogance and selfish behavior tend to turn us away from these people, and we refuse them the kindness that we owe. There are people who have harmed me and my loved ones, so I have no desire to see them prosper. Let your love inspire us. As you prayed for your persecutors, help us to seek relief for our tormenters. Help us see our own weakness, which could easily cause us to harm others. Help us to live at peace with all, to the honor of your name. In your name I ask it. Amen.

273. For Likeness to Christ

Almighty God, you have given us your only Son so that he may be for us both a sacrifice for sin and an example of godly living. Give us grace that we may always receive the priceless gift of his redemption with sincere thankfulness and daily strive to walk in the blessed steps of his most holy life. Amen.

274. For the Holy Spirit

Pour out your Holy Spirit into the hearts of your faithful people, O Lord, so that he may comfort us in our afflictions, guide us into all truth, enlighten us with the gifts of his grace, and kindle in us the fire of his love, according to the promise of your Son, Jesus Christ our Lord. Amen.

275. For a Spirit-Directed Life

Lord God, you give us every good and perfect gift. As your Holy Spirit brings to completion the good work that you have begun in us, help us treasure whatever is true, noble, and right. Preserve us from everything that would provide an occasion for falling into sin. Teach us to live day by day in humble dependence on your promises, in cheerful obedience to your laws, and in sure and certain hope of the resurrection. Strengthen us inwardly with power through your Spirit so that we may abound in love, humility, patience, and prayer until we receive the crown of eternal life, through Jesus Christ our Lord. Amen.

276. To See People Through Jesus' Eyes

O Christ, when you hung upon the cross, you saw the soldiers who nailed you there as those in need of forgiveness. You perceived the spiritual needs of the thief who hung next to you. Your eyes were open to the physical needs of your mother. Blind my eyes to selfishness and greed, envy and jealousy. Give me sight to look at those around me the way that you looked at others so that I may imitate your love in thankfulness for your great salvation. Amen.

277. To Put My Sinful Nature to Death

Dear Holy Spirit, you defeat the desire in me to sin through the power of Word and sacrament. In my sinful nature I so often resist your good work in me. I thank you for my baptism, which tells me that you will never leave me. Keep me from leaving you. Through the power of your Word, cause me to strive against temptation and to rely on the blood of Christ to redeem me. Drown my sinful nature so that I live in righteousness and purity. Amen.

278. To Be More Understanding of Others

"To answer before listening—that is folly and shame" (Proverbs 18:13). God who answers prayer, I do not listen. God of wisdom, I am foolish. God of blameless glory, I am shamefully ignorant of my neighbors' needs, feelings, and points of view. Genuine concern for the welfare of others is so rare (Philippians 2:20); it is rare in my heart too. Change me. Fill me with your love and care. Make my ears as patient, understanding, and open as yours. Amen.

279. To Be a Better Listener

I'm sorry, Lord Jesus, for being so wrapped up in myself. One of the simplest kindnesses I could show to others would be to spend time listening to them, finding out what's on their minds and on their hearts. You spent plenty of your time on this earth listening, even asking questions you already knew the answers to, just to give people a chance to open their hearts to you. I so rarely listen like you. I find certain people tiresome. I don't care how they are. Forgive me. Take hold of my ears. Keep hold of my mouth. Help me serve my neighbors by being a patient, caring, trustworthy listener—like you. Amen.

280. For Divine Guidance

Lord, mercifully direct and guide us in our journey through this life. Although we are surrounded by change and uncertainty, grant that we begin, continue, and end all our works in you; that we may glorify your holy name; and finally, by your grace, be brought safely to your eternal kingdom. Amen.

281. For Wisdom

"Speak, LORD for your servant is listening" (1 Samuel 3:9). That attitude of the young boy Samuel—could you make it my disposition always, Lord? Then I would be constantly listening to your Word and constantly seeking out your commands and heeding your warnings, which will—without fail—keep me from doing what is foolish and will establish my every plan and effort. Here is the only sign I ever need, the only evidence, the only wisdom: that which comes from your Spirit as I meditate on the principles and promises of your Word. Grant it to me in ever-increasing measure, for the sake of Jesus. Amen.

282. For a Humble and Patient Spirit

Lord, do with us as seems best in your own eyes; only give us, we ask, a humble and a patient spirit to wait expectantly for you. Make our service acceptable to you while we live and ourselves ready for you when we die, through your Son, Jesus Christ, our Savior. Amen.

283. For Gentleness

My temper is too short. I am too defensive. I am inconsiderate of other people's feelings. I speak without thinking. I only notice faults, not strengths. Holy Spirit, dove of heaven, you are so gentle with me. You tug at my ornery heart so patiently. You address my unfounded doubts so tenderly. Let me learn gentleness from you. Help me receive the blessing promised to the meek (Matthew 5:5). With the quarrelsome, with the stubborn, with those who would scold me or even despise me—strengthen me to show gentleness to all. Amen.

284. For Joy in All Circumstances

When all seems lost, when life is too hard to live—can I be joyful even then? When I see the righteous mistreated and the commandments scorned—is there joy for me even then? Is there really joy in all circumstances, Lord—joy worth leaping and dancing over? "Restore to me the joy of your salvation" (Psalm 51:12). Yes, restore it to me and let it sustain me through all of life's miscues and messes—the joy of your covenant with sinners, your promises to your children, your unfailing presence, and your eternal kingdom. Give me your Easter joy that no one can take away (John 16:22). Amen.

285. For a Stronger Faith

Dear Father, in your tender love, you have given great and precious promises to your children. Preserve us from the doubts that assail us, and increase our faith. When life puzzles or disturbs us, teach us to fix our eyes on Jesus and to stand firm in the assurance of his promise to uphold and deliver us. We ask this in his name. Amen.

286. For Greater Joy in My Baptism

O Triune God, thank you for transforming me, a sinner, into your own dear child with an eternal inheritance in heaven through Baptism. Heavenly Father, thank you for sacrificing your Son as my Savior. Dearest Jesus, thank you for shedding your blood on the cross to take away my sin and shame. Comforting Spirit, thank you for clothing me in the righteousness of Christ through the washing of water with God's Word. Forgive me for rejoicing so little in the renewal and rebirth you gave me in Baptism. I am sorry I take it for granted almost all the time. Father, Son, and Holy Spirit, never let me forget that I am yours and you are mine through the powerful, cleansing Sacrament of Holy Baptism. Amen.

287. For Greater Joy Over the Lord's Supper

Dear Lord Jesus, although this heavenly meal seems so simple, you have taught me that it is your Supper. Thank you for giving me your body and blood with this bread and wine for the forgiveness of my sins. Thank you for assuring me with this spiritual feast that you have won for me a home of eternal peace. I am sorry that I forget how good this assurance is, how precious this home is. I have such little regard for the communion I enjoy with you, as well as that fellowship I enjoy with like-minded Christians whenever we dine together at your table. Fill me with your grace and satisfy my soul as I eat of the bread and drink of the cup. Help me to delight in this faith-enriching meal from your gracious hand. Amen.

288. For Spiritual Desires

Caring Father, what father gives his child a poisonous snake instead of a fish or a scorpion instead of an egg? Since you care for me, teach me to pray for what you desire. Give me your Holy Spirit through your Word so that I grow in wisdom as I grow in age, just as my brother and Savior, Jesus, did. Keep holy awe and fear of you in my heart, for that is the beginning of wisdom. Amen.

289. For Spiritual Renewal

Almighty and unchanging God, by our baptisms into the death and resurrection of your Son, Jesus Christ, you have redeemed us from spiritual blindness, selfishness, and all dead works. Raise us up in the grace of our baptisms day by day so that we may see you more clearly, love you more dearly, and follow you more nearly, through Christ our Savior, who makes all things new. Amen.

290. For a Purer Life

Holy Spirit, by nature I am the opposite of holy. Day after day I see my sins of lying, lust, and laziness. And I repent of them. But then, the next day, like a dog returning to its vomit, I so often go back to and repeat the same sins I earlier confessed. Like Paul, I cry out, "What a wretched man I am! Who will rescue me from this body that is subject to death?" (Romans 7:24). Before despair conquers me, remind me of my status—completely forgiven— that Jesus won for me. Then strengthen the new person inside me. Strengthen your control over my heart. Amen.

291. For God-Pleasing Prayer

Almighty God, you know our needs even before we ask. Assist us in our prayers so that we may ask only for what is in accordance with your will. Grant us the good things for which we feel unworthy to ask or for which we fail to ask because of our blindness, for the sake of your Son, Jesus Christ our Lord. Amen.

292. For Boldness in Prayer

Heavenly Father, you have invited me to come to you with whatever is on my heart, and you have promised to hear me. You have even promised to give me more than I can ask or imagine. What a wonderful promise, which fills me with hope. When I waver or hesitate to pray, strengthen my faith in your promises. Give me courage to come to you with everything in my life. Make me bold to pray with the confidence that you will hear me and answer my prayers, according to your loving and wise will for me. Amen.

293. For Peace in Serving Jesus

Lord God, all holy desires, all good counsels, and all just works come from you. Give to us, your servants, that peace which the world cannot give so that our hearts may be set to obey your commandments. Defend us also from the fear of our enemies, that we may live in peace and quietness through the merits of Jesus Christ our Savior, who lives and reigns with you and the Holy Spirit, one God, now and forever. Amen.

294. For Grace to Serve (Self-Dedication)

O God, you work in us to will and to act according to your good purpose. Strengthen us in soul and body so that we may do what is pleasing to you and beneficial to all people. Compel us by the self-sacrificing love of Christ and empower us by the gifts of your Holy Spirit to be witnesses of your gospel in our words and in our actions. We ask this in the name of your Son, who came not to be served but to serve and to give his life as a ransom for all (Matthew 20:28). Amen.

295. For a Life of Service

Lord, make me an instrument of your peace:
>   where there is hatred, let me sow love;
>   where there is injury, pardon;
>   where there is doubt, faith;
>   where there is despair, hope;
>   where there is darkness, light;
>   and where there is sadness, joy.
O divine master, grant that I may not so much seek
>   to be consoled, as to console;
>   to be understood, as to understand;
>   to be loved, as to love;
>   for it is in giving that we receive,
>   it is in pardoning that we are pardoned,
>   and it is in dying that we are born to eternal life. Amen.

296. For Zeal to Do God's Work

Too often I put my own concerns and priorities above your will and work, O Lord. Rid me of my selfishness, and fill me with the zeal to keep you first in my life. Amen.

297. For a Blameless Life

Grant me a clean conscience. Where I have sinned, forgive me. When I am tempted, help me remain faithful. Where I am weak, grant me strength. Refresh me in your life-giving, life-renewing grace. Remind me that every good thing I do is really a reflection of your presence with me and your work through me. Grant my conscience peace and rest in your forgiveness as I strive to do what is good and right to your glory with every person and in every situation. Amen.

298. For Use of Talents

Heavenly Father, our Creator, help us put to best use all our talents, abilities, creativity, and imagination in your service. We offer ourselves to you this day, Lord Jesus Christ, our Redeemer; may you control our thoughts, and may we embody your love. We consecrate ourselves to you this day, Holy Spirit, our Counselor; inspire our speaking, sanctify our actions, and cause us to be burning with zeal for you, who with the Father and the Son are one God, now and forever. Amen.

299. For Proper Use of God's Gifts

Gracious God, all that I have comes from you: my body and mind, my strength and intelligence, my time and abilities, my energy and possessions. Guard me from the temptation to use these gifts only for my personal benefit. Make me willing to use them joyfully in service to you and to your people. Amen.

300. Christian Stewardship

All things we have come from and belong to you, O God. Guide us, therefore, to use all we have to the glory of your name and for the good of your kingdom. Take our hearts and fill them with your love; take our lips and move them to speak of Jesus; take our lives and use them to serve in your church. Move us, by the Spirit of Jesus, to do what is needed to spread the gospel of Jesus worldwide for his name's sake. Amen.

301. To Be a Faithful Neighbor

Lord Jesus, you commanded your people, "Love your neighbor as yourself" (Mark 12:31). You have placed me in this world so that I may be a reflection of the faithful love you showed to me by living the perfect life I cannot live and suffering the punishment for my sins. Give me this same attitude of selfless love as I deal with my neighbors: loving them, respecting them, helping them when they're in need, and by my words and actions, being a good witness to them of the love you have for all people. I ask this in your holy name. Amen.

302. To Consider Others More Important Than I Am

"In humility value others above yourselves" (Philippians 2:3). Jesus, when your disciples argued over who was greatest among them, you helped them and me to understand that greatness is defined through loving service to others (Matthew 20:27,28). No one is greater than you, Jesus, who gave your life to save the world from sin. This truth helps me see how important every soul is to you. I see how I can help others by sharing with them how special they are, having been purified from sin by you, Jesus. Together, Lord, you call us all to be your sons and daughters through faith in Jesus. Thank you, Lord, for making every soul important. Help me think humbly of my neighbors' importance. Amen.

303. For Contentment With My Home, My Belongings, and the People in My Life

Lord God, you are the giver of every good gift in my life (James 1:17). Yet, in my sin, I am often unsatisfied and long to have more and better things than you have given. Turn my sinful heart away from selfish gain so that I truly appreciate and rejoice in the abundant blessings you have showered on me: my home, food, clothing, possessions, and the people in my life. Because you have, best of all, given me your Son, my Savior, grant me contentment, joy, and peace in these daily blessings through faith in him. Amen.

304. Ordering a Life Wisely

Make me eagerly desire, O merciful God, those things that are pleasing to you, to the praise and glory of your holy name. Order my life and give me wisdom to know what you would have me do, and enable me to fulfill it. Grant me grace that I may falter neither in prosperity nor in adversity; may I not be unduly lifted up by the one, nor cast down by the other. Let me rejoice only in what leads to you, and grieve only at what leads away from you. Grant me the grace to lament continually my failures, to amend my sinful life, and to direct my heart toward you. Give me a watchful heart that will not be distracted from you by vain thoughts; give me a generous heart that will not be drawn downward by unworthy affections; give me an upright heart that will not be led astray by any perverse intention; give me a strong heart that will not be crushed by any hardship; give me a free heart that will not be enslaved by passion. Bestow on me an understanding that knows you, diligence that seeks you, wisdom that finds you, conversation that is pleasing to you, perseverance that faithfully waits for you, and confidence that embraces you at last. Grant that I may make good use of your gifts in this life by your grace, that I may partake of your joys in the glory of heaven, through Christ our Lord. Amen. (Thomas Aquinas, c. 1225–1274)

305. To Hunger and Thirst for Righteousness

Lord Jesus, you have promised to fill all those who hunger and thirst for righteousness (Matthew 5:6). But my old, sinful flesh constantly craves my own self-righteousness and the false righteousness that the devil and this world offer or the self-indulgence that cares little about what you say is right. If your righteousness does not feed my soul and cover over me, I will certainly starve in my sins and die eternally. Bless me with a heart that always seeks first your kingdom and righteousness (Matthew 6:33) and a faith that longs both for your salvation and for a life of obedience. Let my soul hunger and thirst only for you, because I do "not live on bread alone, but on every word that comes from the mouth of God" (Matthew 4:4). In your name I pray. Amen.

306. For Wisdom in Using My Christian Freedom

Lord God, heavenly Father, as citizens of this country, we are truly blessed! We have the freedom to gather together to worship you without fear of reprisal. We have the freedom to share the saving message that Jesus Christ is the only way to salvation with all those we meet. For these rights and privileges, we give you thanks and praise. We are also thankful, dear Lord, for those who have given their lives so that the people of this great nation might continue to enjoy these freedoms. Lord, may we now seize the opportunities our Christian freedom affords us and work "as long as it is day" (John 9:4) so that more and more may come to know the Messiah's name. Amen.

307. Evangelism

Lord God of our salvation, it is your will that all people come to you through your Son, Jesus Christ. Inspire our witness about him so that all may know the power of his forgiveness and the hope of his resurrection. We pray in his name. Amen.

308. For Courage to Share the Gospel

Give me a caring heart, O Lord, to love and seek the lost. Overcome my fear, and grant me courage to share my hope of salvation with those who have no hope. Make me faithful in my daily life so that all I say and do may glorify you. Amen.

309. For Unity in Faith

God, your infinite love restores those who err, gathers the scattered, and preserves those you have gathered. Heal all divisions, and grant your people true unity of faith so that, nourished by the true Shepherd of the church, they may serve you in all faithfulness, through Jesus Christ our Lord. Amen.

310. To Be More Mindful That Christ Is Coming Soon

Lord Jesus, no one knows the hour of your return, so keep me always watchful and ready for the Last Day. Lead me daily to repent of my sins and live for you by faithfully serving my neighbor in all my vocations. As the signs of the end continue to intensify, take away my fear and let me lift up my head in joyful confidence, for my redemption is close at hand (Luke 21:28). Wake me from spiritual slumber and apathy so that I no longer indulge the sinful deeds of darkness but clothe myself with you and your armor of light (Romans 13:11-14). Come quickly, dear Jesus. Amen.

311. For the Hope of Eternal Life

Lord Jesus Christ, you are the Resurrection and the Life. You have promised that those who believe in you will live, even though they die. Grant to us who live and believe in you the steadfast conviction that we shall not die but fall asleep and on the Last Day, be raised to eternal life. Amen.

Prayers for Personal Goals

312. To Be at a Healthy Weight

Dear Lord God, you are to be praised for providing us with such an abundance of food in our land. Forgive me for the times I have eaten more than is needed or is good for me and for consuming things that are not so healthy. You know how I struggle with my weight. Give me strength to follow a healthy diet and to take time for needed exercise. Lead me to understand that what matters most is not my appearance but my health and a thankful heart. Amen.

313. To Eat Better

Dear Creator and preserver, I know that you desire that I use this body you've given me for your glory and in service to others. How often I have neglected and mistreated this gift by the things I have consumed. How often I have mistreated this temple, which belongs ultimately to you. Forgive me for the sake of Jesus, who always maintained his human body in a perfect and God-pleasing way. Fueled by thanks and love to him, help me to fuel my body with the nutrients needed to function and serve as your child. In Jesus' name. Amen.

314. To Break a Bad Habit

I think I need a friend, Lord—someone to hold me accountable, to help me break my habit of _____. I need more self-control. I need more presence of mind to remember the consequences of continuing this habit. I need your Holy Spirit— send him to fight against my sinful flesh. I have catered to my flesh for too long. I am afraid I won't be able to stop, but I know I should trust in you instead. I don't want this bad habit any longer to get in the way of serving you. Help me tell the people I need to tell, take the steps I need to take, and put to death this foolish behavior. Amen.

315. To Get More Exercise

Dear God, thank you for the gift of physical health. "I praise you because I am fearfully and wonderfully made" (Psalm 139:14). While your primary concern is for our spiritual health, you have also told us that "physical training is of some value" (1 Timothy 4:8). Help me be a wise manager of my physical health. Help me to get more exercise so I have plenty of energy to serve you vigorously. When I put off exercise because there are many things to do, remind me that taking care of my physical health is one of the ways I thank you for saving me. Amen.

316. To Get Organized

Almighty God, when you created this world, you organized and arranged your created work for the good of your creatures. You organize and arrange the affairs of this world by establishing government. In your church you have established order so that there will be peace among your people. As I begin to organize my life (schedule/house/family), keep my priorities focused so that my organizing reflects my faith in your saving work. Amen.

317. To Have Less Stuff

Generous Father, "everything comes from you" (1 Chronicles 29:14). I confess that dissatisfaction, inattention, and bad habits have led me to accumulate more things than I need and to not dispose of things I don't. Forgive my sins of greed and distrust, and renew my heart and mind so that I am not only content with what you give me but glad to keep no more than I need. Grant me, therefore, both discernment and discipline so that both my acquiring and my keeping reflect your values and priorities and not those of my flesh or the world. I ask this for Jesus' sake. Amen.

318. To Get Out of Debt

"The wicked borrow and do not repay" (Psalm 37:21). I don't want to be a wicked borrower. I don't want to leave my creditors in the lurch. Lord, how will I repay them? Give me wisdom in handling money. Keep me strong to earn what I need, both to pay what I owe and to support my family. Keep my priorities straight, so that it is not about financial freedom so much as stewardship of your gifts to me, caring about my neighbor's property and income, and doing what gives you glory. Dear God, faithful owner of all things, help me to abide by your will so that I pay my debts promptly. Amen.

319. To Learn a New Skill

God the Holy Spirit, it was you who gave the skills to the craftspeople who built your holy tabernacle and then the golden temple of Solomon—and I love to imagine how the beauty of those places cheered the hearts of your worshipers. Give me your aid; guide my hands, my body, and my mind; teach me self-discipline and persistence; and grant that I might learn this new skill and use it to cheer the hearts of those who love and fear you. Amen.

320. To Be More Outgoing

Little did the widow of Zarephath know—when she went out to gather firewood one day—that she would meet a very important stranger: a prophet through whom the one true God would keep her family alive in time of famine and raise her little boy back from the dead (1 Kings 17:7-24). The meeting of the widow and the prophet had been prearranged by you, dear Lord (17:9). What strangers would you have me meet, Lord? Who have you prearranged to touch my life with your grace? Help me to stop hiding from the world around me. Make me brave and friendly. I want to meet more people so I can love them as you have loved me, in your Son's name. Amen.

321. To Have More Friends

Heavenly Father, you established a relationship with me in Christ Jesus, even when I loved you not. According to your will, grant me boldness to initiate relationships with others in that same spirit of love, and bless me with the gift of human friendships yet unknown. Amen.

322. To Take More Risks

Open my eyes, Lord, so that I might see how many of your horses and chariots of fire guard my ways all around (2 Kings 6:16,17). I do not need to be afraid. I can do bold, daring things for you and for my neighbors. I can say what needs to be said and stick my neck out for people who need me—all without fear. Neither your promises, your angels, nor your power will ever fail me. Why should I be anxious? "The Spirit God gave us does not make us timid" (2 Timothy 1:7). Purge me of timidity, that I might risk all I am and have for you. Amen.

323. To Spend More Time on People, Less Time on Screens

Almighty Creator and provider, since the beginning you have revealed that it is not good for man to be alone (Genesis 2:18). Though the wonderful gift of technology can bring many blessings to my life, too much time on screens can also isolate me from the family, friends, neighbors, and strangers that you bring into my life for my good. While technology may bring some momentary happiness, friendship with other people provides even greater joy, and by your mercy in Christ I will be able to enjoy these relationships in the eternal life to come. Grant me your grace to always treasure the time you give me with the people in my life. Amen.

324. To Take My Medication When I'm Supposed To

There are times, Lord, when I get fed up with the same routine of taking my prescribed medications day after day. Help me overcome that stubborn and dangerous feeling. Lead me to be grateful for modern medical accomplishments and treatments that can benefit this body you created. Remind me that the doctor has my best intentions in mind and wants me to stay on schedule. Make my medications effective so they will help my health and so I may serve you to the best of my abilities. Amen.

325. To Tell Someone I Need Help

Dear Jesus, self-reliance is good, isn't it? I mean, St. Paul says, "Owe nothing to anyone" (Romans 13:8 New American

Standard Bible [NASB]). I'm often in a "God helps those who help themselves" mind-set. Well, I've taken the Romans passage out of context, and I don't see that second statement anywhere in the Bible. I'm not going to find support in the Bible for my bad habit of not asking for and accepting help when I need it. I do see plenty of passages about helping others in need. And you set the example by helping and healing people in need; you've even raised the dead. In your parable of your coming at the end (Matthew 25:31-46), you even mentioned helping others as a sign of faith in you. Your Word shows me that it's good to help; it's also okay to receive help! I have to admit, "I'm an island, a rock!" and "No, I'm good, thanks!" are often expressions of my sinful pride. By refusing help, I deprive others of their opportunity to serve and, perhaps, myself also of the opportunity to share your gospel with someone you've sent my way. Help me set aside prideful refusal of help. Remind me how graciously you accepted the help of people who supported your ministry. Let me too be thankful for those who come to help. Open my eyes, I pray, to the opportunities you give me to speak of your love with the people you have sent to help me. Amen.

326. To Get Out of a Harmful Relationship

Lord, I remember what you inspired Paul to write: "Do not be misled: 'Bad company corrupts good character'" (1 Corinthians 15:33). The first relationship in my life is you, Lord. My heartfelt prayer is to be closer to you and made more and more like you. I am currently in a difficult and harmful relationship, which, among other things, tempts me to forget you and pulls me away from you. I don't know how to get out of it. I don't know if I'm strong enough to say good-bye. Show me the best way. Help me honor you by saying no to this "bad company." Amen.

327. To Be Able to Express Myself Better

Almighty God, ever since the Tower of Babel, communication has been difficult (Genesis 11:1-9); ever since Eden, it has been tainted with sin (Genesis 3). It can often feel as if I struggle to communicate with others. Send me a rich measure of your Spirit so that I might find the strength to speak up when I must, to speak in love in every situation, and to express myself with clarity so that in everything I think, do, and say, I might bring glory to your holy name. Amen.

Prayers for the Workplace

328. For My Boss

Heavenly Father, in your Word you teach us that we are to respect the authority our employers have over us because they represent you in the workplace. Forgive me for chafing against my boss at times and for sharing my discontent with others. I thank you for providing me with a job and the means of support it provides. Help me to cooperate with my boss and to be a faithful worker. Bless my employer with wisdom and kindness. Keep me mindful that whatever I do in life is my service to you. Amen.

329. A Boss' Prayer

God of truth, Lord and master of all humanity, grant me such completely honest workers that I would hardly need to take an accounting of their labors or their money handling (2 Kings 12:15). Help me treat my employees even better than I would want my boss to treat me. Teach me how to be a servant-leader. Keep me from any kind of pride due to my position. Train my heart to rely on you and you alone in every moment of every workday. Show me how to use my authority not just to make good employees but to "make disciples"—attracting my workers to you by how Christlike I am in all my dealings with them. Amen.

330. For My Coworkers

Lord Jesus, in your wisdom you have made people coworkers with you in proclaiming the message of your salvation. May that knowledge make me humble in my dealings with my own coworkers. Let me express that humility in patience with my coworkers when they annoy me or disagree with me. Let me display that humility in forgiving my coworkers when they wrong me. Above all, let me show kindness toward them so that they may see you through my actions and be led to praise your name. Bless all who work here with me—bless and keep them and make your face shine upon them. Amen.

331. An Employee's Prayer

Lord Jesus, you have redeemed me from sin and by this redemption, have made me to be a new creation in your holy image. Grant that I may daily arise to fulfill your creative will, carrying out my earthly vocation for your glory. Amen.

332. For My Company's Success

Dear Lord, I ask that you would bless the place where I work. This is where I spend so much of my time and effort, and I would love to see my company do well as a result of all the hard work we put into it. Give wisdom to our leaders so that they may direct our business in a way that prospers. Yes, my company's success would bring success to me. But I pray not only that it prospers financially but that it conducts a quality business in a way that is honest and upright. Amen.

333. For Balance Between Work and My Home Life

So many of Israel's godly kings had sons who grew to be wicked kings—what went wrong, Lord? They had it all together when it came to their work in government, it seems, but not in their home life . . . I am frightened by their examples. Balance out my life so that I am faithful both to my family and to my job responsibilities. You made your Old Testament people take days of rest, sometimes even years of rest—when should I rest? When should I work? How can I best show your kind of love to my family, sharing in all their troubles, prayers, and joys? God of rest, God of families, help me. Amen.

334. For Energy for Work

Ever since the fall, work has become hard and daily life a struggle. When I'm tempted to blame my work as the reason for my struggles, remind me that honest work is a good gift from your hand. Renew me with your strength to face the struggles with which sin has infected the good work you've given me to do. Graciously use my struggles to remind me of my constant need for your strength to accomplish the tasks in front of me faithfully and fully. Amen.

335. To Let My Light Shine at Work

My Lord and God, I would consecrate myself to you. I pray that you would make me so holy and kind and sympathetic to my coworkers and my customers that they would ask me about you— that they would give me opportunities to tell of all your wonderful acts (1 Chronicles 16:9). Do not let me hide the lamp of my faith. I want it to shine before others in good deeds, in love like Christ has shown to me (Matthew 5:15,16). Father in heaven, bring glory to yourself through my daily toil. Amen.

336. For Help Dealing With Difficult Personalities

God of peace, you promised to give your servant David "a son who [would] be a man of peace and rest" (1 Chronicles 22:9). So you gave him wise Solomon. And eventually you gave him your own Son as his descendant: Jesus, the Prince of peace (Isaiah 9:6). Give me wisdom and fill me with the knowledge of your Son, that I might also be a person of "peace and rest." You search every heart and understand every desire and every thought (1 Chronicles 28:9): you know how frustrated I get with the people at work, how they drive me crazy and get me so upset. In your kindness, help me see these difficult people with Jesus' eyes of peace. Amen.

337. For Help at My Job to Remember That I Am Serving the Lord, Not Men

Lord Jesus Christ, you had your servant Paul write to Christian slaves, "Serve wholeheartedly, as if you were serving the Lord, not people, because you know that the Lord will reward each one for whatever good they do, whether they are slave or free" (Ephesians 6:7,8). A slave has no choice as to what work to do. A slave receives no paycheck. I am so far from being a slave; how much more ought I to serve wholeheartedly at my work! Keep me from ever forgetting to work hard, not so much for my employer as for you, for your approval, and for your promised rewards, which you grant me by grace. Guide me, your servant, in this way. I want to seek your face. Amen.

338. For a Coworker in Trouble

Lord Jesus, my coworker _____ is experiencing a time of trouble. Enlighten *him* with your Word and lead *him* to see you as the source of all help. Work through me and others to come to *his* aid according to your wisdom and will. Amen.

339. When Work Is Stressful

"They sought God eagerly, and he was found by them. So the Lord gave them rest on every side" (2 Chronicles 15:15). That sounds so good to me, dear God: "rest on every side." Strengthen my heart to seek you eagerly, no matter how stressed out I get. Let my soul find you and find rest in you, even as the workload and work difficulties pile up on every side. May I begin and finish every task with a thankful heart, remembering your kindness. Convince me of your promise— and calm me with it—that my "labor in the Lord is not in vain" (1 Corinthians 15:58). Amen.

340. When Tempted to Disrespect My Supervisor at Work

I am sorry this is even a temptation for me, Lord. Send your Holy Spirit to impress onto my mind the respect you command me to give my supervisor. Make my heart responsive to this your commandment. I would humble myself before you. Save me from this temptation. Watch over me. If it be your will, help my supervisor change *his* bad habits and address the weaknesses I am so quick to notice. But whether *he* changes or even becomes worse, keep me from showing *him* even the slightest hint of defiance or rudeness in gesture, word, or tone of voice. Keep me docile and obedient. Amen.

341. When a Deadline Draws Near

May your hand be on me, O Lord my God, so that I take courage as this deadline draws near at work. Extend your good favor to me before those who will have to judge my accomplishments (Ezra 7:28). Forgive me for any procrastinating I have done and for all the times I have worked on this project carelessly or prayerlessly. I look to you for the strength to concentrate and the wisdom to work efficiently. I want to carry out my responsibilities faithfully—I need you to keep me going. Please give me success. Counting on your mercy, I pray. Amen.

342. When My Company Is Facing a Budget Shortfall

Thank you, Lord, for giving an unending supply of your blessings to us all. I found out that my company is facing a crisis where there is not enough income to cover costs. Please bless those entrusted with management of our company with skills and creative thinking to find solutions to meet the impending fiscal crisis. Help me and my fellow workers to work as productively and efficiently as possible to minimize cost. Lord, hear my prayer and the prayers of others in our company and guide us with good stewardship of the opportunities and work that you have given us as a means to provide for our families and our neighbors in need. As you have blessed us in the past, please continue to bless our efforts according to your grace. Amen.

343. When I Lose My Job

Forgive me, Lord, for whatever I have left undone that would have made me more valuable to my employer. You gave me this job in the first place, and now you have taken it away—don't let this setback make me at all hesitant to praise you. Help me to handle this job loss in such a manner that others would see I have placed my trust in you. As I hunt for a new job—some new way to work for my own daily bread and for the support of my family and my pastor—keep my focus on you. Keep me praying to you about it. Keep me trusting in your great power to provide. Amen.

Prayers for Those in Athletics

344. For My Coaches

Father, you want us to pray for others, so today I am praying for my coaches. Give them the ability to teach athletes well and to do so with patience. Help them to emphasize the positive and be tactful when offering constructive criticism. Let my coaches see the value and needs of each team member, appreciate the important role they have in player development, and keep in mind that each person on the team is more important than any game. Bless them as they put in many hours to help my teammates and me become better at what we do. Amen.

345. A Coach's Prayer

Heavenly Father, we are truly fearfully and wonderfully made (Psalm 139:14)! Thank you for placing these talented athletes under my care. Help me see them not as machines performing precise movements but instead as souls precious to you and loved by you. Draw me again and again to your Holy Word so that I might be an example to them, not only in sports but in life. Whether in games or practice, may I reflect your light to them so that they might see in me something that outlasts human effort and points to the forgiveness you have won for all. Amen.

346. For My Team

Holy Spirit, fill me with the willingness to let my faith shine in the way that I conduct myself as a member of my team. Help me to find the good in my teammates so that I can encourage them. May I use my talents with humility to contribute to our team playing well together. Protect my teammates. Give us focused minds. Help us all to do what we have practiced. Do not let victory become more important to us than conducting ourselves in a way that honors you. Amen.

347. A Player's Prayer

Thank you, Lord Jesus, for my athletic ability and the opportunity to play for my team. Help me to do my best and keep me safe from injury. May I listen to my coaches, cooperate with my teammates, and respect the officials. I also pray that I will play fairly and show respect to our opponent. If it be your will, may we be victorious, but, above all, may we play in a way that brings glory to your name. Amen.

348. For an Injured Teammate

Great Physician, my teammate was injured and needs your healing power. Help *him* through the pain and uncertainty of this new challenge. Bring *him* recovery and strength in due time, if it is your will. Cheer *him* during this disappointing incident and remind *him*, *his* family, and all of us that you love *him* and in all things you work for *his* ultimate good. Lead us, *his* teammates and friends, to be supportive and to continue to pray for *him* as *he* recovers. Amen.

349. For Sportsmanship

Lord, I would like my team to win. But please help each team to use the gifts with which you have blessed them to compete with one another in a spirit of Christian love and to do all things to your glory so that your name may be honored in the world. Amen.

350. For the Refs/Umpires

Blessed Lord, I pray for the referees/umpires in today's game. Give them clear vision, good judgment, and a word of compassion for any athletes who mess up. Protect them from accident and injury, and from the sharp tongues of angry fans and coaches. Let them be honored by every player. Grant them concentration, patience, and impartiality so that all might agree at the end of this game that every call was made just right. Amen.

351. A Trainer's Prayer

Will someone get hurt, Lord, in the next practice, the next workout, the next game, or the next competition? You already know. I pray that no one will. Through quick minds, nimble reflexes, and mighty angels, please keep every one of these athletes in the prime of health. But if you see fit to allow suffering or injury to the players, give me right away the wisdom I will need to help, comfort, and protect them. For those athletes already injured, I pray you would give them patience for all their therapy and hearts that praise you for all healing. Amen.

352. For a Successful Practice

All our strength and all our skills come from you, mighty Creator. The calories we burn and the drinks that keep us hydrated, the self-discipline and teamwork and even the freedom for leisure and sport—all of these are gifts from you. Bless the coaches' plans and the athletes' efforts at today's practice. Let every step and every drop of sweat be to your glory and to the improvement of our team. Keep thanksgiving and encouragement on our lips as we enjoy your gifts of health and camaraderie. You are so generous to us. Thank you! Amen.

353. For Safety

I want to try my hardest, but not test you, Lord. It is not my agility or my padding that protects me. It is only you. Keep us all safe today as we strive and compete. "It is God who arms me with strength and keeps my way secure. He makes my feet like the feet of a deer . . . so that my ankles do not give way" (Psalm 18:32,33,36). Spare us all from hurt and suffering. You are our shield and guardian. Amen.

354. To Give God Glory

"Be exalted, O God, above the heavens; let your glory be over all the earth" (Psalm 57:5). Psalm after psalm proclaims your glory; all creation sings your praise. When we consider the work of your hands, the unfathomable depth of your love, and the undeserved gift of your grace, may our hearts overflow with praise so that in all things—whether in word or deed—we might live lives to your glory, expressing our thanks for all you have done for us. Amen.

355. For God's Will to Be Done, Win or Lose

Grant that more and more each day my will would match yours, dear Lord. When my will isn't in line with yours, help me let go of what I want and enthusiastically embrace what you are doing, trusting that you always do what is good and right and beneficial. Help me live each day with the trust that you will do as you promise, working all things out for my good because you have made me your very own child at the price of the blood of your dear Son! Amen.

Prayers When Facing Temptation

356. In Times of Temptation

You have promised me, O God, that you will never test me more than I am able to bear. So I turn to you in my weakness and ask for strength to resist and overcome the temptations so often placed in my path by Satan and my sinful flesh. Teach me through your Holy Word to desire what is right in your eyes and cause me to live a life of daily repentance, looking to Jesus for pardon and strength. Amen.

357. For Protection Against the Devil

Lord Jesus, you suffered the temptation of Satan in our place and defeated him for us. You have given us the power to rise above the temptations of the evil one. In our daily struggle against the spiritual forces of darkness and in our inner battle with our sinful nature, shield us with your divine protection. Strengthen us with your grace so that we may stand firm in every temptation and finally overcome and obtain the victory. Amen.

358. For Faithfulness to God

Dear ever-faithful Lord and God, I need your help at every moment. There are so many things that vie for my attention and time. Often I find that they try to lead me away from faithfulness to you. Help me to fight against Satan's attempts to draw me away from my allegiance to you and your Word. Focus me on Jesus and the unfailing faithfulness he has shown and always will show to me. "If we are faithless, he remains faithful, for he cannot disown himself" (2 Timothy 2:13). By your gospel lead me to always remain faithful to you, in response to your faithfulness to me. In the name of my faithful Savior, Jesus. Amen.

359. For Strength of Heart

Give me, O Lord, a steadfast heart, which no unworthy affection may drag downward; give me an unconquered heart, which no tribulation can wear out; give me an upright heart, which no unworthy purpose may tempt aside. Bestow on me also,

O Lord, my God, understanding to know you, diligence to
seek you, wisdom to find you, and a faithfulness that may
finally embrace you; through Jesus Christ our Lord. Amen.
(Thomas Aquinas, c. 1225–1274)

360. For Godly Internet Use

Almighty and eternal God, you have created us in your image
and have directed us to seek after all that is good, true, and
beautiful, especially in the divine person of your Son, our Lord
Jesus Christ. Grant that during our use of the Internet, we will
direct our hands and eyes only to that which is pleasing to you
and treat with charity and patience all those souls we encounter,
through Christ our Lord. Amen.

361. For Help in Withstanding Current Worldly Attacks

Heavenly Father, just as a fish is not aware of the water in which
it swims, so we can become insensible to the harm the world
can do to our souls. As you teach us in your Word, the world
rejoices in the cravings of sinful man, the lust of his eyes, and the
boasting of what he has and does (1 John 2:16). So that the values
of the world will not overtake me, I pray that you would lead me
to take up "the sword of the Spirit, which is the word of God"
(Ephesians 6:17), to defend myself against these attacks. Amen.

362. For an Accurate Conscience

Order my footsteps by thy Word and make my heart sincere;
let sin have no dominion, Lord, but keep my conscience clear.
Assist my soul, too apt to stray, a stricter watch to keep; and
should I e'er forget thy way, restore thy wandering sheep.
(Isaac Watts)

363. When Tempted to Love Something More Than God

Heavenly Father, when I am tempted to love and enjoy the
things you have given me in this life, remind me that you are
my highest joy. Do not let me enjoy the things of this world
as ends in themselves, but rather let me use them almost
absentmindedly, as one whose tunnel vision craves incessantly

for the full enjoyment of eternal life with you. "Those who use the things of this world" should only use them "as if not engrossed in them" (1 Corinthians 7:31). Keep my eyes fixed on you, without whom nothing brings any real or lasting joy. Amen.

364. When Tempted to Fear Something More Than God

"The eyes of the LORD are on those who fear him" (Psalm 33:18)—I want your eyes to be on me, Lord. "Fear the LORD, you his holy people, for those who fear him lack nothing" (Psalm 34:9)—I long for that promise to be mine so that I might "lack nothing." Impress these passages on my heart. The fear of missing out on this world's pleasures and promises or this world's approval, the fear of losing this world's good things—none of this should matter to me. None of those things can save or preserve me. "It is you alone who are to be feared" (Psalm 76:7). Amen.

365. When Tempted to Not Trust God

Lord God, heavenly Father, like Adam and Eve in the garden I am tempted to not put my trust in you. When I am enticed to doubt, remind me of your faithfulness to Adam and Eve and every generation. When I'm uncertain of your faithfulness, show me again how your promises have always proven trustworthy. Drive doubt from my heart and replace it with humble trust in your goodness and grace. I ask this in the name of him who is the ultimate proof of your faithful love for me, Jesus my Savior. Amen.

366. When Tempted to Despair

"My thoughts trouble me and I am distraught" (Psalm 55:2). I am thinking about giving up. I don't want to wait for you anymore to make things better. I feel like there isn't any hope. "Record my misery; list my tears on your scroll—are they not in your record?" (Psalm 56:8). I know you keep track of my every sorrow and tear, every tremble of my heart. Help me. Give my mind relief. "My eyes fail, looking for my God" (Psalm 69:3). Please stop hiding. I need to know your grace again. I need reassurance that your Son is still at my side. Amen.

367. When Tempted to Doubt a Bible Passage

Forgive me, Lord, my failures to trust all that you reveal to us in Scripture. Help me keep in mind the awesome promise you spoke, saying, "I have called you friends, for everything that I learned from my Father I have made known to you" (John 15:15). May I never doubt your love by thinking that you have withheld from me something I need to know in order to live now and forever with you in heaven. When I need more understanding of a Bible passage, guide me in the study of Scripture to find other passages that will enlighten your meaning to me. Give me humble, childlike faith. I thank you, Lord, every day for the truth that sets me free from sin and guides me to eternal life in Jesus. Amen.

368. When I Keep Forgetting to Pray

I forget your power. I forget your covenant promises. I forget how much I need your deliverance. I put you to the test by charging ahead into my life without seeking your blessing. The psalm writer prays to you, "Pour out your wrath on . . . the kingdoms that do not call on your name" (Psalm 79:6). But so often, like the unbelieving nations, I do not call on your name, Lord. Train my stubborn tongue. Make me like David, who could say, "I call to you all day long" (Psalm 86:3) and, "I am a man of prayer" (Psalm 109:4). I say to you what your Son's disciples said: "Lord, teach us to pray" (Luke 11:1). Amen.

369. When I'm Not Sure Prayer Is Worthwhile

Dear Lord, forgive my doubting. It is senseless of me to even halfway despise the privilege of prayer, the honor of an audience before your throne. It must be offensive to you that I would question your promises to hear and answer me for Jesus' sake. But I do have questions and doubts. I'm sorry, but I don't know how to make the doubts be quiet. Reconvince me. Reinstill in my spirit the childlike trust a dear little one has in a loving father. "Christ Jesus who died—more than that, who was raised to life—is at the right hand of God and is also interceding for us" (Romans 8:34).

Engrave the beauty of my Savior's intercessions on the eyes of my heart. I want to mean it every time I say, "Amen."

370. When Tempted to Despise My Pastor's Preaching

Am I joining the arrogant, Lord? "Their hearts are callous and unfeeling," the psalmist says, "but I delight in your law" (Psalm 119:70). I have lost my feelings of delight in listening to my pastor preach your law. My heart has become callous to my pastor's pronouncements of forgiveness and your love. Am I so arrogant as to think I have heard it all before or there is nothing your called servant can teach me? Renew my joy to "go to the house of the LORD" (Psalm 122:1). Open my ears again to the wonders of your mercy. Let my pastor's preaching be my very bread and breath, even my song in the night. Amen.

371. When Tempted to Despise My Parents

Lord God, you have given me my parents as a blessing to care for my body and soul. Help me not to forget the ways in which they have done this but to be thankful for their every act of love. Through them you guard and keep me for eternal life. As your Son honored both his heavenly Father and his earthly father and mother, help me to honor mine. Amen.

372. That I Might Not Sin in My Anger

O Lord, I know myself. I know how easy it is for me to sin when I get angry. Sometimes I just lose it. I also know what you have said—that I should not sin in my anger. Forgive me when I sin in anger. By the power of that forgiveness, empower me to hold my tongue and keep me from sinning. I can't do this without you. I ask you to strengthen me, and I trust you to help me. Amen.

373. That I Might Forgive

Your forgiving love endures forever, Lord. Mine can hardly get started. I am slow to trust in your justice, slow to believe you will repay the wrongs of all who hurt your children. I feel like I cannot rest until I know just how everything will be made right again. This isn't how you want my heart to be. This shows how little I appreciate how you have forgiven me. Yes, I am "nearsighted and blind, forgetting that [I] have been cleansed from [my] past sins" (2 Peter 1:9). Have pity on me. Save me from my own vindictiveness. Put into my heart the love that "covers over a multitude of sins" (1 Peter 4:8). Amen.

374. When I Don't Want to Help Someone in Need

"A generous person will prosper; whoever refreshes others will be refreshed" (Proverbs 11:25). Lord, I don't want to be generous right now. Help me trust your promise that this is the path to refreshment. "Whoever is kind to the needy honors God [their Maker]" (Proverbs 14:31). Help me care about honoring you. "If anyone has material possessions and sees a brother or sister in need but has no pity on them, how can the love of God be in that person?" (1 John 3:17). Put your love in me, dear God, and fill my heart with pity. Amen.

375. When I Don't Want to Be Friendly

"Do not be proud, but be willing to associate with people of low position" (Romans 12:16). My unfriendliness is proof of pride. Give me humility instead, Lord Jesus. "An unfriendly person pursues selfish ends" (Proverbs 18:1). My unfriendliness is proof of selfishness. Give me a generous servant heart instead, Lord Jesus. You befriended me when my only friend was the flames of hell. You gave your life for me when all I could do was despise you. Grant that I would fear and love you enough to be the friend my neighbor needs. Amen.

376. When Considering Divorce

Why can't I see the good qualities in my spouse anymore? Why can't I remember what I used to love in *him*? Why is it so hard to say kind things to my own *husband*? Can't we even enjoy each other's company? Lord God, you taught me to love you when I hated your every word: teach me to love my *husband* again. Rebuild our mutual trust. Rekindle our mutual affection. Give us a love that our neighbors and family "rejoice and delight" to see (Song of Songs 1:4), like they rejoiced at our wedding day. Save our marriage, dear Father, and save my heart. Amen.

377. That I Might Flee From Sexual Immorality

Dear God, you have given men and women the gift of sexual relations to serve us as an unselfish blessing. I live in a world where that gift has been twisted and warped to manipulate and take advantage of others. When I am bombarded by sinful sexual images, thoughts, or situations, Lord, help me to run away from them and to you. Give me a heart that seeks your ways. Give me eyes that look for you and your will. Give me the desire to do what is pleasing to you. Then, when I find myself tempted to lust, remind me of your promises; when my desire burns, help me to overcome it; and when I fail and I sin, forgive me and set me free from the twin dangers of helpless, guilty shame and calloused indifference. My hope is in Jesus, my Redeemer and Savior. I pray in his name. Amen.

378. When Tempted to Take Advantage of Someone

The elderly, the lonely, the defenseless, the children, the foreigner, the poor, those with disability, the unsuspecting, naive, and simple—these are the people you have put into my life to especially love and serve. Again and again in Scripture you say that you pay particular attention to these people and how they are treated. "In their sad accents of distress your pleading voice is heard; you may in them be clothed and fed and visited and cheered" (CW 524:3). Put to death, Lord, my cold-heartedness. "Why not rather be wronged? Why not rather be cheated?" (1 Corinthians 6:7). Make me generous to all so that I would rather be taken advantage of myself. Amen.

379. When Tempted to Gossip

Lord Jesus, it is written, "Consider what a great forest is set on fire by a small spark. The tongue also is a fire, a world of evil among the parts of the body" (James 3:5,6). When I hear rumor or truth about someone else, help me to speak only in love. If my brother or sister sins, move me to "go and point out their fault, just between the two" of us (Matthew 18:15). Thank you for speaking well of me before the throne of your Father in heaven. Amen.

380. That I Might Take My Neighbor's Words and Actions in the Kindest Possible Way

Dear Holy Spirit, giver and protector of my faith, thank you for counseling me and leading me by the truth of your Word. You have brought me to see Jesus as my Lord and Savior. You continue to strengthen my faith so I see how I can lead a godly life, especially toward others. Help me overcome drawing any quick assumptions about what others say about me or do to me. As you have been patient with me, lead me to be patient with others in Christian love. Please lead me to see the great benefit there is in protecting the reputation of others (and my own reputation by guarding my tongue). In the name of Jesus, my Savior. Amen.

381. When Tempted to Lust

You, LORD, you yourself are my strength and my defense (Isaiah 12:2). Defend me against my own eyes, my own perverse imagination, and my own lustful heart. Strengthen me to say with righteous Job, "I made a covenant with my eyes not to look lustfully" (31:1). Remind me that the house of adultery is "a highway to the grave" (Proverbs 7:27). Fill me with holy dread of being kept outside the gates of your golden city along with "the sexually immoral . . . and everyone who loves and practices falsehood" (Revelation 22:15). Forgive my lusts, purify me from them, and show me a better way to use my time and my eyes. Amen.

382. When I Am Not Content

"Let us eat and drink, . . . for tomorrow we die!" (Isaiah 22:13). This is sinful unbelief: to try to get as much worldly pleasure and possessions and affection as we can as if there is no eternity, as if we have no souls. Exalted and eternal Lord, give my soul rest from greed and gluttony. Place my hopes upon your everlasting feast—in my heavenly, imperishable home. "We

rought nothing into the world, and we can take nothing out
of it. But if we have food and clothing, we will be content with
that" (1 Timothy 6:7,8). Amen.

83. When I Don't Want to Do What Is Right

thank you, Lord, for your patient forgiveness. Too often I am
stubborn and ignore what you say is right. Help me, Lord, and
continue to call out to me to stop my sinful rebellion. I know a
momentary indulgence of a sin has the potential of leading me
away from you forever, Lord. I find myself too often like the first
son in the parable you told, Jesus (Matthew 21:28-31), saying I'll
follow you but not following through. So rule my heart, Lord,
that in the end I will second-guess my every desire to sin against
your will and instead desire to do what you so lovingly ask of
me. Help me toward this goal so that I honor and praise you,
Lord, with all my thoughts, words, and actions. Amen.

384. When I've Been Taking My Baptism for Granted

Lord, I confess to you that I too easily forget whose I am. You
named me as your own dear child in the waters of Baptism.
Forgive me for failing to reflect on the rich treasures that are
mine because I have been baptized into your family. Help me to
reflect on all you give me because you have called me your own
through the blood of Christ. Lead me to rejoice daily in all that
this means: I am a baptized child of the Most High God! Amen.

385. When I Don't Find Much Meaning in the Lord's Supper Anymore

My God, open my eyes to see how desperate my sinful condition
is. Unstop my ears to hear how much your Son loves me. What
am I basing my confidence on? What makes me think I am so
rich and so righteous that I no longer hunger—like the wretched
beggar that I am—for this richest and miraculous food? I am
afraid of how little your Son's body and blood mean to me
lately. Overtake me with gladness and joy—how gracious that
my filthy lips should be allowed to touch the body of heaven's

King! Here is strength for the weary and power for the weak. Empower my weak spirit to love this Supper again. Amen.

386. When Tempted to Despise My Pastor's Words of Absolution

No other god even knows who I am. No other religion can offer me even a single word or answer from heaven or any consolation over my many, many sins. You are the only God, and without your forgiveness, I am doomed and damned. Why doesn't this mean more to me? You should sweep me away into hell, not least on account of how smugly I view your commandments and the afflictions of your Son. But instead you give me a pastor who speaks to me as with your own mighty voice and says, "I have swept away your offenses like a cloud, your sins like the morning mist" (Isaiah 44:22). Soften my hard heart to your grace. Amen.

387. When Tempted to Despise Those in Government

Lord, the authorities that exist have been established by you. As you have given the church your Word for the eternal good of your people, you have also given authority to the state for our temporal welfare. Help me to show respect for your servants and to hold them and their office in the highest regard. Amen.

388. When Tempted to Resent My Elders

"This is what the high and exalted One says—he who lives forever, whose name is holy: 'I live in a high and holy place, but also with the . . . lowly. . . . These are the ones I look on with favor: those who are humble and contrite in spirit'" (Isaiah 57:15; 66:2). High and exalted One, I need to be much more humble, especially toward those older and wiser than I am. "Submit yourselves to your elders," the apostle Peter commands (1 Peter 5:5). May the promise of your presence and your favor strengthen me to humbly honor my elders in all things. Amen.

Prayers Regarding God's Promises

389. All Things Work for My Good

My loving and faithful God, you promise in your Word that in all things, you work for the good of those who love you. You have called me into your kingdom through faith in Christ as my Savior. So I claim this promise and ask that you would keep me mindful of it. Help me to also see that not only pleasant things are good for me and to understand that hardships and difficulties can serve for my eternal good. Amen.

390. Blessings to All Who Keep His Commandments

By our sins, heavenly Father, we forfeit your blessings and should hear nothing but wrath in your commandments. But your obedient Son covers us with his perfect life of love. Yes, and he covers up all the sinful stains on our acts of obedience and love. Now we hear your commandments as the guidance of a loving parent, kindly making promises to entice the children to listen. Repeatedly, you promise that you are gladly watching and ready to reward—in your grace for the sake of Christ—our every attempt to serve you. Use these promises to increase my zeal to serve. Amen.

391. Daily Bread

Dear preserver, thank you for providing for all my needs. I do not deserve the rich blessings you have bestowed on me. I confess my greed, wanting more than daily bread. I confess that at times I am never content with your gracious blessings. As you bless me with food, clothing, shelter, and all I need for body and life, bless me also with faith to ask only for what I need day by day. Help me rest in your care and be content with what you give me. Amen.

392. God Disciplines Those He Loves

Heavenly Father, how incredible your love is for me that you should call me your child. Help me realize that your love for me includes disciplining me for my good. Keep me from spurning your corrective care and lead me to understand that your discipline comes from a heart that longs for me to place my hope in you alone. Give me a humble heart and submissive spirit to see your discipline not as a burden but as a blessing that will result in a firmer trust in you. Amen.

393. God Is an Ever-Present Help

"God is our refuge and strength, an ever-present help in trouble. Therefore we will not fear" (Psalm 46:1,2). Is the earth giving way? Your help will not give way. Are the mountains falling into the heart of the sea? No waves can sweep my help and strength away from me. Are the nations in uproar, the kingdoms falling, the earth melting? The refuge you provide me is guarded by heaven's angel armies. It rests upon the unshakable foundation of your Son's name. "My help comes from the LORD, the Maker of heaven and earth" (Psalm 121:2)! Amen.

394. God Is Love

Heavenly Father, so often the devil twists and warps the definition of the word *love*. In our sinful world, *love* is thought of as tolerance for or condoning of anything and everything that people use to indulge their sinful nature. We often are tempted to believe that our loving God wouldn't let his people suffer. We are told that it is unloving to insist that your law is the standard by which we and all people should live our lives. Forgive us for these errors and turn us to your Word, where we find that your love is your mercy to sinners who deserve only your wrath. Because you are love, you sent Jesus as our Savior from sin so that, by faith in him, we have eternal life. We thank you for your mercy and love in Jesus' name. Amen.

395. God's Kingdom Cannot Be Stopped

Lord of kings and nations, you uproot mighty kingdoms more easily than I dig up dandelions. The poorest throne you establish so none can topple it. The promised days have come. You have raised up for David's line a King who does what is just and right (Jeremiah 23:5). His kingdom "will never be destroyed" (Daniel 2:44). However many turn from the faith and let their love grow cold, however many nations and demons rise up against Christ, the "gospel of the kingdom will be preached in the whole world" (Matthew 24:10-14). May I ever praise you for bringing me into your unstoppable kingdom! Amen.

396. God's Will Is Always Done

"Sovereign LORD, you have made the heavens and the earth by your great power and outstretched arm. Nothing is too hard for you. You show love to thousands but bring the punishment for the parents' sins into the laps of their children after them. Great and mighty God, whose name is the LORD Almighty, great are your purposes and mighty are your deeds" (Jeremiah 32:17-19). You have shown so much love to me. You have promised to carry out such great purposes in my life *and the lives of my baptized children*. I know that no one can hold back your hand (Daniel 4:35). I gladly and eagerly wait to see your loving will be done, for Jesus' sake. Amen.

397. God Won't Give Me More Than I Can Bear

Lord, like the prophets of old who spoke in your name and like your servant Job, help me to be an example of patience in the face of suffering. Lead me to trust that my present sufferings are not worth comparing with the glory that will be revealed in me. When temptation comes, help me to follow the way out that you have provided, according to your Word. Let me fix my eyes on Jesus, the pioneer and perfecter of faith, who for the joy set before him endured the cross, scorning its shame, and sat down at the right hand of the throne of God. As I run the race marked out for me, let my patient endurance bring you glory in the church and in the world. Amen.

398. My Father Knows What I Need Before I Ask Him

"When you pray, do not keep on babbling like pagans, for they think they will be heard because of their many words. Do not be like them, for your Father knows what you need before you ask him" (Matthew 6:7,8). Considering how skimpy my prayers can be, how confused my priorities get, and how blind I can be to my own condition, I am truly blessed to have a Father who knows what I need far better and far sooner than I do—yet who is still happy to hear even my feeblest prayers. Thank you, kind Father. Amen.

399. My Labor in the Lord Is Not in Vain

I thank you, O God, who has given us victory over every enemy through our Lord Jesus Christ for the privilege of laboring in this world to serve you, your church, and my fellow man. There are times when my service seems unappreciated or unfruitful. There are days as I live out my calling when grumbling comes more easily than joy or fear leads to inaction. Forgive my unfaithfulness, and send your Holy Spirit every day to strengthen my heart and mind's grip on your promises so that my labor in the Lord is not in vain and that rewards of grace await me in heaven. Amen.

400. My Redeemer Lives

"[My] Redeemer is strong; the LORD Almighty is his name. He will vigorously defend [my] cause so that he may bring [me] rest" (Jeremiah 50:34). His tears have dried, his torments ended, his grave is empty—he lives! "I know that my redeemer lives, and that in the end he will stand on the earth. I myself will see him with my own eyes" (Job 19:25,27). He lives and he will never forget me. He will never stop protecting me from my old cruel masters who would reclaim me. Jesus Christ my Redeemer lives and "is the same yesterday and today and forever" (Hebrews 13:8). Amen.

401. My Tears Are All Numbered

"Though he brings grief, he will show compassion, so great is his unfailing love" (Lamentations 3:32). Is this grief somehow a gift from you, dear Father? I wait for you to show compassion: Show that you feel this grief right along with me, show me this has hurt you too. "List my tears on your scroll—are they not in your record?" (Psalm 56:8) The way I've been crying lately, I'm sure you've had to keep that scroll nearby. Have you cried too, while you record my every tear? I know you have already noted what number the last tear will be. Comfort me, Father. Amen.

402. Rest for the Weary

Jesus, my troubles are too great for me to bear. Yet you entered the world for this very purpose. You came not just to take sin upon yourself but also to carry all my infirmities and sorrows. Lord, I relinquish them all into your strong arms to carry away. Yet more than that, I place myself into your loving arms and trust that you will work out everything for my good. If it is your will, you will remove my burdens. If not, you will keep me from being overwhelmed as I trust that your power is magnified in my weakness. Help me find rest in you, knowing that, by your grace, I am truly strong and able to overcome all things. Amen.

403. The Holy Spirit Is Praying With Me

"The Spirit helps us in our weakness. We do not know what we ought to pray for, but the Spirit himself intercedes for us through wordless groans. And he who searches our hearts knows the mind of the Spirit, because the Spirit intercedes for God's people in accordance with the will of God" (Romans 8:26,27). The Spirit you poured generously into my heart at my baptism: Whenever I pray, he prays with me! It is truly wonderful. Yes, "he can plead for me with sighings that are not speakable by lips defiled" (CW 189:4). How confident I can be whenever I say, "Amen!"

404. The Lord Is My Shepherd

Dear Good Shepherd, help me make the words of David my own (Psalm 23). Lead me to confess with conviction that you alone are my sufficient Shepherd. Your shepherd's love moved you to lay down your life for me. I thank you. Remind me of your promise to lead me into good pastures and to feed my soul with your satisfying Word. Quench my thirst with your quiet message of gospel peace. Guide and guard me through this life, protecting me from the attacks of the wily foe until I come to the perfect peace of paradise. In your name. Amen.

405. There Is Nothing to Fear

O most loving Father, you want us to give thanks for all things, to fear nothing except losing you, and to lay all our cares on you, knowing that you care for us. Protect us from faithless fears and worldly anxieties, and grant that no clouds in this mortal life may hide from us the light of your immortal love shown us in your Son, Jesus Christ our Lord. Amen.

406. The Return of Christ

Lord Jesus, you have promised your church that you will soon return in glory to deliver us from all our troubles and sorrows. We long for your appearing and pray, Come, Lord Jesus! We rejoice that you have shortened these perilous last days for the sake of your elect. For that mercy, we thank you! And when you come, grant that we may be found faithful, trusting in the salvation you have given us and making good use of our time of grace. Come quickly, Lord Jesus! Amen.

Prayers for Personal Trials

407. For a Refuge

We pray to you, almighty God, in this time of _____.
Be our refuge and our strength, an ever-present help in time of
trouble. Do not let us lose courage in the face of these events.
Uphold us with your love, and give us the strength we need.
Help us in our confusion, and guide our actions. Heal the hurt,
console the bereaved and afflicted, protect the innocent and
helpless, and deliver any who are still in peril. For the sake of
your great mercy, in Jesus Christ our Lord. Amen.

408. For Eyes Fixed on Jesus

Heavenly Father, ever since the beginning, Satan has been
directing human eyes away from you and your Word and
toward his lies and accusations. But now, in my trials and
temptations, fix my eyes only on your Son, Jesus Christ,
because it was his joy to endure the cross for my sake
(Hebrews 12:2). He destroyed the work of the devil (1 John
3:8) and is not ashamed to call us his brothers and sisters
(Hebrews 2:11). In every tribulation and affliction, let me
always see Jesus—the strength of my heart, the joy of my life,
and the hope of my salvation. In his name I pray. Amen.

409. For Confidence in Trouble

Dear Lord of the Church, you warned me about the cost I must
pay for being your disciple. You told me to take up my cross and
follow you. Yet the road is difficult. Give me courage to bear the
difficulties that come into my life. When troubles go on and on
and I am tempted to despair of ever receiving your help, have
mercy on me and give me relief. When you decide to turn my
time of trouble into a time of relief, may my first thought be to
praise and honor you, O Lord. Amen.

410. Bearing the Cross

Dear Lord, who joyfully bore the cross so that we might not have
to bear the eternal pain of God's wrath, strengthen us as we bear

our crosses in this world. Too often we selfishly desire that you would simply take our crosses away. Instead, lead us to pray for stronger backs to carry the crosses we do have. Forgive us for the times we have held a grudge against you for allowing this or that cross into our lives. Help us see our crosses as evidence of your deep love for us. Teach us to always find our peace in you—you who promised to give rest to the weary. Merciful God, according to your will and at your time, take our crosses from us and bring us to yourself in heaven. Amen.

411. In Great Distress

When I am in distress, dear Lord, I think of you. I ask you to listen to the cry of my heart. I neither can nor will prescribe the time and the way in which my distress might be removed. I will wait for you to determine the when and how of my relief. Strengthen my faith and give me patience to bear my trouble so that at last I may be glad when you visit me with your grace and remove my distress. Dear Father, you have never forsaken your children; do not forsake me now. You cheer the hearts of your despairing children; lift me up at your appointed time. I leave all to your wisdom, love, understanding, and goodness. Amen.

412. In the Dark Hours

Lord God, your Word tells me that "we look for light, but all is darkness; for brightness, but we walk in deep shadows" (Isaiah 59:9). As your Word reminds me, the darkness that drains me and the cold that crushes me are not from seasons or weather. Instead, it's the sin in my heart. In my darkness, give me through your Word what guessing intellect and slippery emotions cannot give: the strength of your forgiveness and the promise of your presence. Amen.

413. In Times of Need

Lord God, you know our human weaknesses and frailties. You know our needs and cares. We do not in any way deserve your help, Lord, but we truly need it. Therefore, we come to you in this time of need. Grant us peace of mind so that we may face the difficulties that now confront us. Strengthen our weak faith, lead us with your strong right hand, and work things out so that they serve our eternal good. In Jesus' name. Amen.

414. In Pain

Dear Lord Jesus, my pain is almost greater than I can bear. Sometimes it makes me very afraid. Have mercy on me, I pray. Watch over me, and let your healing hand rest on me. Then I will not be afraid but patiently await the day when you will take my pain away. If it is your will, let that day come soon. Hear me, Lord Jesus, and help me. Amen.

415. In Anxiety

Consider, soul, the birds above,
Who do not reap or store;
Lord, free my soul to trust your love,
And trusting you, to soar. Amen.

416. In Depression

Dear Jesus, I am depressed, and sometimes this sadness is overwhelming. Lift my spirits. Focus my attention on the cross, where I see your amazing love for me. Help me to see that even in my sadness, your mercies are new to me every morning. Give me strength to cope with the troubles and sadness in my life. Help me to find joy in my relationships. Renew in my life a purpose to live for you and serve you in all I do. Amen.

417. When Life Seems Pointless

O Holy Spirit, with King Solomon I find myself saying, "Meaningless! Meaningless! . . . Utterly meaningless! Everything is meaningless!" (Ecclesiastes 1:2). As you revived the king, so I pray, revive me. Show me the joy and purpose of following my Lord Jesus, who is "the way and the truth and the life" (John 14:6). He has redeemed me from sin so I have life with him. May I enjoy the abundant life he has won for me by living it to the full. Amen.

418. Feeling Useless

I feel useless, Lord. Unmissed. Unneeded. Like the people of Israel in exile saying, "Our bones are dried up and our hope is gone" (Ezekiel 37:11). But in Baptism you brought my dry bones to life. You made my heart a temple where your glory dwells, from which rivers of living water gush forth (John 7:38). You hold in your hand my life and all my ways (Daniel 5:23). As I prayerfully carry out my Christian duties, I reveal your glory to the world, whether I can notice it or not. Help me believe this and find my usefulness in you. Amen.

419. When Sick

Great Physician of body and soul, I have been struggling with sickness and pain. If it is your will, let these days pass quickly. Guide the hands of those who care for me, and give me confidence in their skills. If I must continue to suffer, grant me the comfort of knowing that you will allow nothing to happen to me that is not for my eternal good. Amen.

420. When Sickness Reminds Me of My Sins

O God, my gracious Father in Christ, you have told us that your loving purpose in permitting affliction to come on your children is to draw them closer to you. I humbly and gratefully acknowledge that you have been my rock and refuge from the moment I was taken ill. Yet, as the hours wear on into days, I am deeply troubled by the thoughts of doubt and the feeling of despair that threaten me because of the weakness of my faith. O faithful Father, sustain me in my trial. Strengthen my faith. Do not let me be tempted above what I am able to bear. Do not let me doubt your love or question your wisdom in permitting this affliction to test and try me. Relieve my pain or, if it is your will that I should bear it longer, give me the necessary strength to endure it. Fulfill your promise in me: "I will be with you; I will never leave you nor forsake you." Grant my prayer, O Lord, for the sake of your beloved Son, my only Savior Jesus Christ. Amen.

421. For Patience in Sickness

O God, the Father of our Lord Jesus Christ, in whose grace there is strength to act and patience to endure, you have relieved us in all our distresses; you have sustained us in times of despair; in many ways you have blessed us day by day. Help us now to follow you to the end. Give us strength to conquer hopeless brooding and irritable impatience. Give your servant the ability and the desire to cooperate with those who are providing care. Grant that my faith may be so strengthened and hope confirmed that I may never openly complain nor secretly murmur against you. If I face depression, grant that with the eye of faith, I may see you with unclouded vision, remember your past mercies, and be encouraged to hope that you will refresh my soul. Help me to believe that in times of discouragement, your grace will sustain me; that even in illness, you will help me. Give me faith to believe that though recovery is slow, in all things you work for the good of those who love you. Sanctify my days and bring peaceful nights so that I may be restored to health and strength, through Jesus Christ, our Lord. Amen.

422. After Receiving Bad News From the Doctor

"My times are in your hands" (Psalm 31:15), dear Lord. You know the length of my days. My heart is heavy because of the hard news my doctor has shared. Lord, you know discouragement and difficulty because you walked through extremely dark times in your life here on this earth. You promise you are with me always, even now in this dark valley. Though Satan tempts me to be down and discouraged, lift my spirits with your presence and your promises. Though "my flesh and my heart may fail" (Psalm 73:26), Lord, strengthen me to find my hope and joy in you! Amen.

423. After a Serious Accident

Lord God, heavenly Father, you know what is in my mind and heart as again and again I relive the frightening experience that has left me bruised in body and dazed in spirit. Sustain my faith so that I may trust your love and wisdom, even if I do not now understand. If it is your will, grant me a speedy recovery. All healing power comes from you alone. In your mercy you have spared my life for a purpose. Guide me by your Holy Spirit so that I may make the most of the time that you have granted me by dedicating myself to serving you and the people around me. To your gracious care I entrust my body and soul. In Jesus' name. Amen.

424. In Physical Therapy

Lord Jesus, when you walked on earth, you provided healing to many who suffered from various physical ailments. Now, from your throne on high, you provide your loving care through medical professionals, whom you have blessed to be a blessing to others. As I work with my therapist to recover physical abilities that have been diminished, give me patience and perseverance. And if it is your will, allow me to regain the gift of good health. No matter the outcome, fill my heart with trust in your loving care. Amen.

425. When Death Seems Near

Lord Jesus, you have promised, "Heaven and earth will pass away, but my words will never pass away" (Matthew 24:35; Mark 13:31; Luke 21:33). In my affliction I sense that all earthly things are passing away from me. Your Word alone stands firm. In it I am assured that you have "redeemed me, a lost and condemned creature, purchased and won me from all sins, from death, and from the power of the devil, not with gold or silver but with [your] holy, precious blood and with [your] innocent suffering and death" (Luther's Small Catechism, Explanation to the Second Article of the Apostles' Creed). O loving Savior, help me to cling to you in steadfast faith until you make your promise come true to me: "Today you will be with me in paradise" (Luke 23:43). Into your almighty hands I commend my body and soul, now and forever. Amen.

426. For Bravery in the Face of Death

Like Daniel thrown into the lions' den, keep me brave, O living God, great Ancient of Days. Why should I fear death? It is but a "sleep in the dust in the earth" from which I will awake to "shine like the brightness of the heavens" (Daniel 12:2,3). It is but my passage into paradise, with my eagerly waiting King. "Where, O death, are your plagues? Where, O grave, is your destruction?" (Hosea 13:14) Like a hornet that has lost its sting, death can only buzz at me. My Savior has conquered it, and he promises me, "Whoever obeys my word will never see death" (John 8:51). Keep me brave to the end, which is really the beginning of complete joy. Amen.

427. Before Surgery

Heavenly Father, as I face surgery, I am passing through troubled waters in my life. How thankful I am, even in this difficult hour, for your promises to be with me and to protect me. Be with my surgeon and all who assist. Preserve my life, and grant an outcome in accord with your will. I confidently place myself into your hands, for you are my faithful and merciful God. Amen.

428. During an Extended Stay at the Hospital

Lord, I do not fully see where the path before me leads. Bless the care that I am receiving so that I may be restored to better health. Help me to be patient and trusting, even in the lonely hours of the night. Most important, strengthen and keep me in the one true faith that looks to Jesus Christ for forgiveness, life, and salvation. Restore my soul through your Word and Sacrament, and bless those who carry them to me during these days. Amen.

429. Thanksgiving for Recovery

Gracious Father in heaven, your mercies are new every morning and your faithfulness every night. I called you in my sickness, and you sent comfort and relief. You gave knowledge and skill to the doctors and nurses who attended me. With your help I am now well on the road to recovery. Let me never forget your undeserved goodness toward me. Fill my heart with genuine gratitude. Help me from this day to live a godly life, always remembering your loving admonition: "Do not love the world or anything in the world. . . . The world and its desires

pass away, but whoever does the will of God lives forever"
(1 John 2:15,17). Grant me this precious blessing, through Jesus
Christ our Lord. Amen.

430. When My Pet Is Sick

Creator of everyone and all things, my dear pet is sick
and it makes me feel anxious and sad. Thank you for the
companionship of my animal friend and the joy it brings me. I
know you care about all your creatures. If it is your will, allow
my pet to improve and get better soon. Help me make the best
decisions I can to help in that healing process, always applying
good stewardship principles and considering the advice of the
people who know what best should be done. Amen.

431. After My Pet Has Died

Lord of all life, not even a sparrow falls to the ground without
your knowledge (Matthew 10:29). We mourn the loss of our
beloved pet. This animal was an instrument of joy through
which you regularly brightened our days on this earth. Thank
you for the companionship with which you blessed us through
him. As we sorrow over our loss, help us to see the seriousness of
sin, which has condemned the natural world to decay and death,
so that we may once more marvel at your love for us that would
send your Son for fallen mankind. Amen.

432. When There Is Strife

O Lord, it grieves me that anger, strife, and bitterness have
become a part of my life. Forgive my sins and renew my spirit
so that I will pardon others, correct the mistakes I have made,
and be more cheerful toward those around me. Remind me
through your Word that your Son's peace provides the needed
hope and reason for healing and change. Amen.

433. In Loneliness

Merciful God, in my anxiousness and loneliness I turn to you.
You alone can calm me and give me the strength I need to
face the troubles and challenges of each new day. Place your

everlasting arms under me, and make me unafraid. Hold me up, and teach me to follow as you lead. Bring me at last to the safe haven of eternal peace you have prepared for your believers in heaven. Amen.

434. When Uncertain What to Do

O Lord our God, we need your guidance in all we do. Let your wisdom counsel us, your hand lead us, and your arm support us. Conform us to your image, and make us like our Savior so that in some measure, we may live here on earth as he lived and may act in all things as he acted, through Jesus Christ our Lord. Amen.

435. Fear of Tomorrow

O heavenly Father, you know all about us. You know our past and our present. You know what our future holds. Even though we do not know what it holds, it is enough to know that you love us. In quietness and confidence, we place our lives in your hands. Strengthen our faith, and help us to understand your everlasting love. Cause us to have the peace of God, which transcends all understanding. We pray in the name of Jesus. Amen.

436. A Restless Heart

I know my soul can only find rest in you (Psalm 62:1,5), trustworthy God. But I cannot seem to find that rest right now. I know your Son promises me rest for my soul, if I only bring him my burdens and weariness (Matthew 11:28,29). But I cannot seem to let my burdens go. Creator of rest, Lord of the Sabbath-rest, you made provision even for the rest of the donkeys and the oxen of Israel (Exodus 23:12). I pray you put to rest my restless, untamed heart. Amen.

437. A Sleepless Night

"He who made the Pleiades and Orion, who turns midnight into dawn and darkens day into night . . . the LORD is his name" (Amos 5:8). You, O LORD, are the untiring, unchanging I AM. You "neither slumber nor sleep" (Psalm 121:4). All night you keep earth spinning and constellations shining. You send dreams into the minds of kings and beggars. I know you are awake right now to hear me pray. And I know your promise: "He grants sleep to those he loves" (Psalm 127:2). You will give me sleep at the right time. Till then, let my every thought be of your unchanging beauty. Amen.

438. Before a Big Speech or Performance

Creator of minds and mouths, you have promised that in these last days you "will purify the lips of the peoples" (Zephaniah 3:9). Your Son paid with his blood to make me a holy priest (Revelation 1:6). Purify my lips. Help me to speak like the holiest of Israel's priests: "True instruction was in his mouth and nothing false was found on his lips" (Malachi 2:6). I have learned my words and studied my lines. Guide my tongue and bless me so that I might glorify you with my every breath and touch every heart with beauty and truth. Amen.

439. When the Nights and Days Are Long

Blessed Lord Jesus, I cry out to you from the depths of loneliness and despair. Help me to pass the weary hours of the night and the heavy hours of the day. Through your redeeming power, lift up my heart and grant me the knowledge that however desolate the hour, I am not alone, "for you are with me; your rod and your staff, they comfort me" (Psalm 23:4). When no one seems to care, help me to remember your everlasting love. O Savior of the world, save me from the loneliness of this world and take me at last to be with you and all your saints in heaven. Amen.

440. When I Don't Know Why God Hasn't Taken Me to Heaven Yet

Lord, the hymn writer states, "I'm but a stranger here, Heaven is my home. Earth is a desert drear, Heaven is my home" (CW 417:1). Lord, I'm ready to come home. The joys of heaven await and I long to be with loved ones who have gone before me. But I also know that it isn't time until you call my name. Forgive me for growing impatient and for losing sight of my purpose. For you have revealed that the reason you keep me here is always this: There is someone who does not yet know that you are "the way and the truth and the life" (John 14:6). Lord, help me trust that you are using me to be a blessing to others, even if I never see the results. Grant me the grace to persevere until you decide it is time for me to come home. Amen.

441. Considering Suicide

Lord of my life, forgive me for not trusting you with my life. Strengthen my weak faith, and help me commit my way to you each day. Drive all depressing thoughts from my heart, and encourage me with your life-giving promises. Help me to thankfully live the life you have restored for me in loving service to you and to others. Hear me for your mercy's sake. Amen.

442. Car Trouble

Lord Jesus, you tell me not to worry about food and clothing. Surely you would tell me just the same about my car: to not worry. How much will the repairs cost? You have that figured out, and how I'll pay the bill too. How messed up will my day or my week be because I can't count on my car? You have that under control. You teach the tiny hummingbird how to cross continents and oceans; you can get me where I need to be with or without a car. Please fix my car, but most of all, fix my faith on you. Amen.

443. When Someone Is Telling Rumors About Me

Dear Lord Jesus, my reputation is precious to me. I want people to think well of me, and I try to give a positive impression to all I meet. But some people try to build themselves up by tearing others down. Rumor-telling and gossiping are popular activities that provide negative entertainment for willing ears. Help me to live and speak in a way that will contradict the rumors. Give me the opportunity to address in a positive way the person spreading the rumors. And show me how to respond without spreading rumors in return. In your name, I ask it. Amen.

444. When I Think I Am Unworthy to Go to Communion

Dear Lord Jesus, I have sinned and do not deserve to receive your body and blood at your table. I may appear to be as good as the others who are communing today. But I do not want to add hypocrisy to my guilt, which you can see when others cannot. Help me to overcome my guilt. Help me to understand that you gave your body and blood not for the righteous but for sinners. Give me faith to trust your grace, no matter how great my sin may be. And grant me again the peace that your Sacrament was designed to give. In your name, I ask it. Amen.

445. When My Faith Is Being Tested

When you tested Abraham, asking him to sacrifice his beloved son Isaac to you, at the last minute you provided a ram to take Isaac's place (Genesis 22). Will it soon be the last minute of my time of testing? Until then, grant me the confidence of Job, who said, "He knows the way that I take; when he has tested me, I will come forth as gold" (Job 23:10). You are refining me like silver (Psalm 66:10), proving genuine my faith—"of greater worth than gold, which perishes even though refined by fire" (1 Peter 1:7). Please let the test be brief. In the name of Christ, the tested and precious cornerstone (Isaiah 28:16). Amen.

446. When I Have Lost Someone's Trust

I'm sorry, Lord, for not being trustworthy and considerate. All the times I have failed and disappointed _____, I also failed and grieved you. Forgive me. Do not forsake me. Show me the path to re-earning _____'s trust. You restored your disciples' trust in you when they had completely given up on you. Yes, your resurrection is the beginning of the restoration of all things. Please may it be your will to restore the trust I have lost. Make me dependable again. Amen.

447. For Strength to Tell Someone Something They Don't Want to Hear

I need the courage of John the Baptist, Lord, who rebuked wicked Herod for his sins, even though John ended up being beheaded for it. I need your own courage, dear Jesus—you who called out the hypocrisy of the chief priests, the teachers of the law, and the elders. But I also need your gentleness, your sympathy for weak sinners, and your steadfast calm. Anoint my lips with your Spirit. Use my words to help my friend. Amen.

448. For a Fresh Start

Dear gracious giver of this new day, you remind me in your Word that your mercy is new every morning (Lamentations 3:22,23). You encourage me to rejoice today, for it is the day you have made (Psalm 118:24). I've made such a mess of things. If only I could do things over. I am consumed and paralyzed with regret and remorse. Focus me on the cleansing power of Jesus' blood. Remind me that my past is forgiven and my future is in your good hands. Help me to live this day with joy in my heart, starting fresh as your redeemed child. In Jesus' name. Amen.

Prayers for Others Facing Trials

449. For Others in General

Lord God, hear me as I speak to you about those near and dear:
> For all who travel: Keep them safe.
> For all who are sick: Heal them and make them strong.
> For all who are in pain: Allow them to have relief.
> For all who are discouraged: Let someone bring them cheer.
> For all who mourn losses: Grant them understanding
> and recovery.
> For all who feel their hopes have been dashed through
> death: Be the strong arm they need through Christ, who
> suffered death and rose again.

Dear Lord, let them know that nothing can separate them from your love in Christ Jesus. Amen.

450. Concern for Others

Dear Lord of all creation, you have promised to care for the needs of your people. Help us share your concern, especially for those who are undergoing problems in this life. Help us encourage those who are victims of the sins of others. Help us show compassion to the sick and injured. Help us identify those who have special needs, and give us the desire to go out of our way to help them. Keep the example of your Son, Jesus, always before our eyes as one who gave up all he had in order to serve us. Amen.

451. For the Sick

Dear Creator and preserver of life, frailties of body and soul plague each of us. Today I come to you on behalf of those who are confined to sickbeds. If it is your will, ease their pain, restore their health, and allow them to return to their daily activities according to your gracious timetable. Enable them to see in their sickness an opportunity to give glory to you. Because you sent Jesus to take away the lasting effects of sin and disease, comfort these people with the timeless message of your love. Renew in them the certain hope of eternal life. And grant them all joy in living now and in eternity, for Jesus' sake. Amen.

452. For a Sick Person (Adult)

Compassionate Father, in your mercy you transform even sickness and disease into a blessing for your children. With this confidence we commit all who are sick or suffering to your tender care. We pray especially for _____. Provide healing and relief according to your infinite wisdom and boundless mercy. Grant patient endurance if *his* suffering must linger. Help *him* find true spiritual strength through Jesus and his cross during this time of physical weakness. By the work of the Holy Spirit, teach *him* to trust in your forgiveness, grace, and love. In Jesus' name, we pray. Amen.

453. For a Sick Person (Child)

Lord Jesus, in your Word you assure us that our children are dear to you. Have mercy on this sick child, for whom we offer our prayers. Spare the life that you have given, and grant healing and recovery according to your will. Comfort the parents who watch over their little one with the assurance that their child is also your child, purchased with your blood and made a member of your spiritual family through Baptism. You have promised never to forsake your own. Therefore, we commend this child into your loving hands, knowing that there *he* is safe today, tomorrow, and forever. Amen.

454. For One Who Is in Trouble

O blessed Lord, God of mercies and comfort, look with compassion on your servant _____, who is shaken and troubled. In your good time, give *him* a right understanding of himself and your will for him so that *he* may not lose confidence in you. Preserve *him* from bitterness and fear, look on *him* with favor, and give *him* your peace, which transcends all understanding, through your Son, Jesus Christ our Lord. Amen.

455. For the Distressed

Almighty God, the consolation of the sorrowful and the strength of the weak, hear the prayers of those who cry out to you in sickness or sorrow, in trouble or distress. Grant relief to those suffering pain, comfort to those who mourn, and recovery to those burdened by illness and disease. Look with compassion on the homeless, the destitute, those whose inner hurts we cannot see, and all who have none to care for them. Soothe and heal all who are broken in body or spirit, and bring us all to the perfect peace and rest of heaven, for the sake of Jesus, your Son and our Savior. Amen.

456. For Those Facing Tragedy

God of compassion, you watch our ways, and out of terrible happenings you weave wonders of goodness and grace. Surround those who have been shaken by tragedy with a vivid sense of your love, and keep them strong in faith. Though they are lost in grief, may they find you and be comforted; through Jesus Christ, who was dead, but now lives and rules with you over all creation. Amen.

457. For One in Time of Need

It would not be any trouble for you, Lord Jesus, to help in this time of need. I do not consider myself worthy even to bring this request before you. But for my friend's sake I cannot be silent. Say the word and the need will be addressed (Luke 7:6,7): it will be met so generously, it will seem like the need was never there. Have pity on this friend, as you did on all who brought their needs to you while you walked this earth. Please, Lord, do not turn this request away. Amen.

458. For One Who Is Suffering

Our loving Father, we come to you in the name of our Savior, who suffered so much for us. We have confidence that our needs are known to you and that out of the abundance of your mercy, those needs are met. Watch over your child and protect *him* in *his* hour of weakness. May *he* be sustained by faith in the assurance of your nearness and love. Grant that in *his* suffering, *he* might be a faithful witness to all your loving purposes. This we pray, together with our unspoken prayers, in the name of Jesus our Savior. Amen.

459. For Someone in Pain

Our Father, we thank you for the mercy of our Lord Jesus Christ and the way in which he endured human pain. Sustain your servant in *his* hour of trial so that by your grace, *he* may have courage. Give *him* patience, and in your good time grant *him* release from *his* pain. Help *him* to know that you are ever by *his* side. Sustain *him* with the confidence that in all things you work for our good, through Jesus Christ our Lord. Amen.

460. For One Who Has Been Injured in an Accident

Gracious Father, in your wisdom you have permitted your servant _____ to be injured in an accident. While we do not fully understand your purpose in allowing this to take place, we are assured by your Word that in all things, you work for the good of your children. We thank you for sparing *his* life and pray that you would permit *him* to recover from *his* injuries. Give *him* patience and a faith that humbly and thankfully submits to your will and direction each day, for the sake of Jesus our Savior. Amen.

461. For the Family of an Accident Victim

Almighty and merciful Father in heaven, look with compassion on those whose hearts are heavy with anxiety for their loved one who has had a serious accident. Have mercy on *him*, and when it pleases you, grant *him* deliverance. Bestow on *his* dear ones grace to endure this time of uncertainty with courage and serenity. Strengthen them in the confidence that you will do what is best both for them and for *him*. In Jesus' name, we pray. Amen.

462. For Someone Facing Surgery

Merciful Lord and Savior, you have promised to be with your believers everywhere and in all circumstances of life. May the assurance of your abiding presence and loving care comfort and

sustain your servant _____ as *he* faces and undergoes
surgery. Remove all anxiety and fear from *his* heart, and lead
him to rest all *his* confidence in you. Bless the work of the
surgeon, and give success to the surgery as it pleases you. Be
with _____ as *he* recovers, and fill *him* with an abiding
thankfulness for all your blessings. Amen.

463. For Absent Ones

O God of mercy and might, we ask you to turn your eyes with
favor upon our dear ones who are absent. Shield them from all
physical harm. Guard them against all dangers to their souls.
Keep them strong and true in faith in Jesus Christ, your Son and
our Savior, in whose name we pray. Amen.

464. For Someone Near Death

Eternal Father, you alone make the decisions about life and
death. We implore your mercy on _____, whose
departure from this life seems near at hand. As *he* passes
through the valley of the shadow of death, comfort *him* with
faith's assurance that you are with *him* and that *he* need not be
overcome by fear. Spare *him* extreme physical pain. Encourage
him and *his* loved ones with the sure hope of the glory that you
have prepared for your believers in heaven. Into your hands
we commit *him*, O Lord, our Redeemer. Amen.

465. For Those Who Mourn a Death (Adult)

O Lord God, Lord of life and death, we thank you for all
the mercies with which you blessed our fellow believer
_____, now fallen asleep. We thank you especially for
having brought *him* to the knowledge of your Son, Jesus Christ.
We pray that you would comfort *his* family and all who mourn
his death with your precious promises, and cheer them with the
sure hope of a blessed reunion in heaven. Grant the lifeless body
rest and at last, together with us all, a joyful resurrection to life
everlasting. Teach us to number our days aright so that we may
gain hearts of wisdom and finally be saved, through Jesus Christ,
our risen and ever-living Lord. Amen.

466. For Those Who Mourn a Death (Child)

Almighty and everlasting God, with Job we declare, "The LORD gave and the LORD has taken away; may the name of the LORD be praised" (1:21). In your merciful love, you gave this child to *his* parents. In your infinite wisdom, you have taken *him* from *his* earthly home to *his* eternal home. Although we do not always understand your ways, help us to humbly follow you as you lead us through life. Help us put our trust in your unfailing love. Comfort the parents who have suffered this grievous loss—and all who mourn with them—with the assurance that through Holy Baptism, _____was delivered from sin and is forever safe with you in glory. Lead us all to look forward eagerly to the day when we will be reunited with those who have gone before us and will see you face-to-face in heaven. Hear us, help us, and bless us for Jesus' sake. Amen.

467. For the Parents of a Stillborn Child or a Child Who Has Died Shortly After Birth

O Lord our God, your ways are often hidden, unsearchable, and beyond our understanding. For reasons we cannot comprehend, you have turned the joyful hopes of these parents into sadness. We know, dear Lord, that your ways are loving and wise. But we are often confused and fearful. Help those who now experience sorrow to bow humbly before your will. Comfort them with your life-giving promise that in all things you are working for their good. Amen.

468. For Those Who Suffer Miscarriage

O gracious Lord, you have not revealed why some children die before birth. Yet we know that you moved John to leap in his mother's womb with joyful faith. You lovingly hear Christian parents who pray for their unborn children. Cause pregnant mothers to be regular in their worship attendance, recognizing that your blessing spoken in the worship service also reaches living babies in the womb. Comfort those who suffer loss, and empower us to trust you. Amen.

469. For Those Who Mourn a Death (Suicide)

Dearest Jesus, many hearts are breaking with this loss that we do not understand. We may never understand. Help the grieving to know that you are the God whose love for them and their loved one is higher than the heavens are above the earth and to know that you send their sins as far away as the east is from the west. Relieve whatever guilt they may be carrying, and comfort them with your love. Give them strength to go on from here and face each day knowing that you love them. Amen.

470. For Those Who Mourn a Death (Murder)

"Out of the depths I cry to you, LORD; Lord, hear my voice" (Psalm 130:1,2). Since the moment I heard about this shocking death, I have been thinking about the bereaved loved ones and the agony they must be feeling. I can hardly believe that this terrible thing has happened. Help the grieving to learn to cope with this and even to bring your comfort to those around them who join them in their grief. Have mercy on the soul of the one who did this, for Jesus' sake. Put your forgiving love into every heart. Amen.

471. For Those Who Mourn a Death (Questionable Circumstances)

Risen Lord Jesus, you know what is in each person (John 2:25). You know the grief these mourners are now feeling, their confusion, and their every question. Comfort them, just as you comforted your grieving, confused disciples. "Why are you troubled," you asked them, "and why do doubts rise in your minds?" (Luke 24:38)—not because you didn't know the answers, but so that your great victory over death could drive away their troubled doubts. May all who mourn this disturbing death take all their griefs to you, Lord. Reassure them, through and through. Amen.

472. For the Family at the Death of an Unbelieving or Heterodox Family Member

Lord of love, we remember in our prayers the family of
_____, who has been taken from them by death. We ask
that you would give them the strength they need in this time of
grief, and comfort them with the precious assurance of your love
for them in Christ Jesus. May this death remind us all of how
quickly our lives here on earth come to an end. Lead us all to use
the time you have given us to grow in our knowledge of you and
your Word. When you summon us, may we be found in sincere
repentance and steadfast faith, prepared to stand before your
judgment seat through the merits and righteousness of Jesus the
Savior. Amen.

473. For Nursing Homes

Dear Lord, send your blessings on those living in long-term
healthcare facilities and nursing homes. When the days become
long, give the residents patience. When their roommates become
a source of irritation, give them inner peace that lets them rise
above the annoyances. When there seems to be so little cheer,
give them the hope and peace that your Word alone can give.
Bless your Word in the hearts of the residents and compensate
for the physical abilities you have taken away with a rich
measure of spiritual strength and joy. Amen.

474. For the Poor and Neglected

Almighty and most merciful God, hear us as we pray for the
poor, the homeless, the neglected, and the outcasts of society.
Remind us that you often choose those who are poor in the
eyes of the world to be rich in faith. Move us to speak up for
the destitute and the oppressed and to relieve their distress.
Lead us to reach out in love and compassion to those who are
unloved, unlovely, forsaken, or forgotten. Grant this through the
intercession of your Son, Jesus Christ, who for our sake became
poor. Amen.

475. For the Homeless

Dear Father, Maker and giver of all I have, this evening I will fall asleep well-fed and tucked under warm blankets with a soft pillow under my head. I know full well that many people do not have these simple, much-needed blessings. That is why I come to you on behalf of those who are sleeping in places of discomfort and even danger. Keep them safe this night. Help them find rest wherever they might lay their heads. In the morning lead them to find something to eat. Lead me to be generous with the blessings you have given me to help those in need, nearby me and far away. Most of all, may the gospel of my Savior also warm the hearts of the homeless with the grace and mercy you freely give. In Jesus' saving name. Amen.

476. For Immigrants

Lord Jesus, you made Abraham the immigrant glad (John 8:56). You prepare a place in heaven for all your disciples (John 14:2,3), including those who have no place to call their own here on earth. Really, we Christians are all immigrants "not of the world any more than [you are] of the world" (John 17:14). The crowd you saved at Pentecost was made of visitors from many other lands. Fill us and our fellow citizens with sympathy for all immigrants. Let them be treated fairly and with hospitality. Above all, use the churches of our land to make these immigrant visitors glad with your salvation. Amen.

477. For the Unemployed

Heavenly Father, you have given dignity and value to honest labor. We commend to your care all who are unemployed and unable to find satisfying work. Do not forget or forsake them. Keep them from bitterness and frustration, and help them cast their cares on you. Graciously supply their physical needs from day to day. Encourage them as they seek work, and in your mercy increase the opportunities for employment in our land. Give us all the spirit of love that willingly bears one another's burdens and shows itself in genuine concern for one another's needs, for the sake of Jesus, whose compassion never fails. Amen.

478. For Prisoners

Lord Jesus, for our sake you were condemned as a criminal. Look with mercy on all prisoners. Lead those who are guilty to repentance and amendment of life. When any are held unjustly, bring them swift release. Since what we do for those in prison, O Lord, we do for you, lead us to show true concern for them and to act in their best interest. Hear us for the sake of your loving-kindness. Amen.

479. For Addicts

O blessed Jesus, you ministered to all who came to you. Look with compassion on all who, through addiction, have lost their health and freedom. Restore to them the assurance of your unfailing mercy; remove the fears that attack them; strengthen them in the work of their recovery; and to those who care for them, give patient understanding and persevering love, for your mercy's sake. Amen.

480. For Travelers

Dear Lord, be with those who are traveling. Keep them from harm and danger. Keep their cars trouble-free, protect them from careless drivers, and give them quick reflexes to respond to potential problems. Keep the planes and trains in your hand, and make them safe modes of transportation. Should we be involved in an accident, protect us from serious harm. Especially be with our young people who are traveling to and from school. Keep them safe in all their activities and use your mighty angels to protect them from danger. Give us an extra measure of protection when the weather is bad. Prompt us to thank you daily for your help. Amen.

481. For Widows

O God, my prayer rises to you in your holy habitation. I pray for widows everywhere, but especially those who belong to your family of faith: Protect them from everyone who might take advantage of them and defend them from every danger or disadvantage that might make their days more difficult. In their grief, grant them comfort in Christ and the resurrection; in their loneliness, grant them first joy in your presence and then delight in the presence of faithful people who will love and delight in them in turn. I ask this in the name of Christ, their Savior. Amen.

482. For Those Tempted by the Lies of Evolution

Dear Father in heaven, we cannot see you, but we love you. We also cannot always see how you have done everything you have done. But help us all to believe all that you have told us—how you created the world and everything in it in seven ordinary days and especially how you sent your Son to save us from the sin that has ruined the world you created. It took Spirit-given faith for ancient people to trust your creating and saving power, and it takes Spirit-given faith for modern people to do the same. Remind us all that we can never be smarter than the book of Genesis and that while scientists' theories come and go, your Word stands sure and certain forever. Amen.

483. For Those Tempted by Homosexual Desires

Gracious Lord, when King David asked you, "Create in me a pure heart" (Psalm 51:10), his was not a momentary or temporary request. And his request was not unique to him either. As I pray for those who struggle against homosexual desires, I join David and all your people in continually asking you to give me, but also all these strugglers, pure hearts—graciously give the strength to live as the new creation in Christ Jesus you in your grace intend for them to be. Help all who face these temptations to focus on "whatever is true, whatever is noble, whatever is right, whatever is pure, whatever is lovely, whatever is admirable" (Philippians 4:8). Amen.

484. For Those Working in the Porn Industry

Christ Jesus, as Paul preached in the "sin city" of Corinth, in a holy vision you reassured him, "I have many people in this city" (Acts 18:10). "Many people"! Corinth had a thousand "sacred prostitutes": it was a city renowned for debauchery and sex trafficking. But you had "many people" there: many sinners written in your book of life, soon to be redeemed and washed clean of all their sins. Friend of sinners, I pray that among those shaming and debasing themselves in the production of pornographic materials even today you would "have many people." Send them redemption. Wash them clean. Purify their hearts by faith. Amen.

485. For Friends Who Do Not Go to Church

Good Shepherd, friend of sinners. Your heart of compassion led you to reach out to the lost and the wandering. You know the dear people in my life who are not following you. My heart longs for them to know the joy and peace that come from hearing your voice and following where you lead. According to your gracious will, give me openings to share the saving gospel with them. Keep me from being a stumbling block to them. Prepare me to always be ready to share with them the reason for the hope that I have. Amen.

486. For the Members of Non-Christian Religions

Living Messenger of light, please hear my prayer on behalf of all members of non-Christian religions. You died for them too. You have ready for them, this very moment, the life-purpose and salvation they crave from their false teachers and false gods. "Open their eyes and turn them from darkness to light, and from the power of Satan to God, so that they may receive forgiveness of sins and a place among those who are sanctified by faith in" you (Acts 26:18). Amen.

487. For the Members of Churches That Teach Falsely

The night before you died, dear Jesus, you prayed for unity among all your followers—as perfect as the unity you enjoy with your Father (John 17:22,23). It's hard to see how that prayer of yours has come true. Teachers serving their own appetites "deceive the minds of naive people" (Romans 16:18). Call these teachers back to the truth. Cleanse all preaching from error. Sharpen the discernment of all churchgoers to reject additions to and subtractions from your Word—reject them as

poison and disease to their souls. Christ, you are not divided
(1 Corinthians 1:13): Heal the divisions in your body. Amen.

488. For People Who Have Been Hurt by the Church

Lord Jesus, your kingdom, the church, is made perfect by your
blood. Until you come again in glory to end this sinful world,
however, the churches that we can see are populated by sinners
who too often hurt their brothers and sisters. Especially painful
is when your people are hurt by those who you have placed over
them as leaders in the churches. Be with these victims of sin and
comfort them with your love. In your mercy, heal their spiritual
and emotional wounds. Work in their hearts so that they may
hear your Word and be led to forgive those who have sinned
against them and be restored to confidence in your holy Church.
In your name we pray. Amen.

489. For Those Who Have Forgotten Their Baptism

Loving Father, like children playing outside are reminded,
"Don't get your nice clothes dirty," remind all baptized
Christians that their baptism clothed them with Christ
(Galatians 3:27). Like a child who wants a bedtime snack is
reminded, "You already brushed your teeth," remind them that
Christ has cleansed them by the washing with water through
the word (Ephesians 5:26). Like a person complaining in the
hospital is reminded, "You're lucky you're alive," remind them
that in Baptism, they were buried and raised to life with Christ,
in whose name I pray. Amen.

490. For Those Whose Consciences Are Distressed

God of all judgment, God of all pardons, it is frightening when
we get a glimpse of how despicable our sins against you really
are or a sense of your utter holiness. I pray to you for those who
can't get past their terror of your wrath, those weighed down
by guilt, those despairing of forgiveness. "Here is a trustworthy
saying that deserves full acceptance: Christ Jesus came into the
world to save sinners" (1 Timothy 1:15). Dear God, lead these

troubled consciences to fully accept and trust that saying and to find in it complete peace. Amen.

491. For Those Who Think They Have No Sins

"When you judge the law, you are not keeping it, but sitting in judgment on it" (James 4:11). So many people judge your law to be easy, even beneath them—Holy Spirit, help them really see what it says. "If we claim we have not sinned, we make him out to be a liar and his word is not in us" (1 John 1:10). So many people see themselves as "basically good"—Holy Spirit, put into their minds and hearts your humbling and delivering Word. Show all people the ugliness of their disobedience so that they might know the beauty of the Savior's scars. Amen.

492. For Those Who Are Under Attack Spiritually

"The accuser of our brothers and sisters, who accuses them before our God day and night, . . . [he] is filled with fury, because he knows that his time is short" (Revelation 12:10,12). He is "enraged" and "wage[s] war against . . . those who keep God's commands and hold fast their testimony about Jesus" (Revelation 12:17). You have already triumphed over him, King Messiah. Put all your people out of the accuser's reach. Shield them from his fury and rage. Drown out all his accusations with songs of the blood of the Lamb. Fill the hearts of all your embattled saints with loud hallelujahs and with the certainty of your love. Amen.

493. For Open Doors and Open Hearts Toward the Gospel

Lord Jesus, it is your will that all people come to a knowledge of the truth of your gospel and be saved (1 Timothy 2:4). Throw aside the efforts of Satan to close doors to your saving message. Provide more and more opportunities for your Word to be preached throughout the world. Send out an army of faithful witnesses of your Good News. Open my heart to sharing your message. Open the hearts of all who hear, and through the work of your Holy Spirit in their hearts, bring them to faith in you. Amen.

494. For Everyone

Dear lover and Redeemer of every soul, I pray for everyone. Although I won't know the smallest percentage of them, I hope to see them in your eternal kingdom one day. Be with your people in every land so that your gospel message of peace in Jesus might reach everyone. Send your gospel to every land so that your Spirit might break through the night of unbelief with the sunshine of faith in Jesus. Give our world true peace, joy, hope, and unity through your powerful Word. In the name of Jesus, friend and Savior of all. Amen.

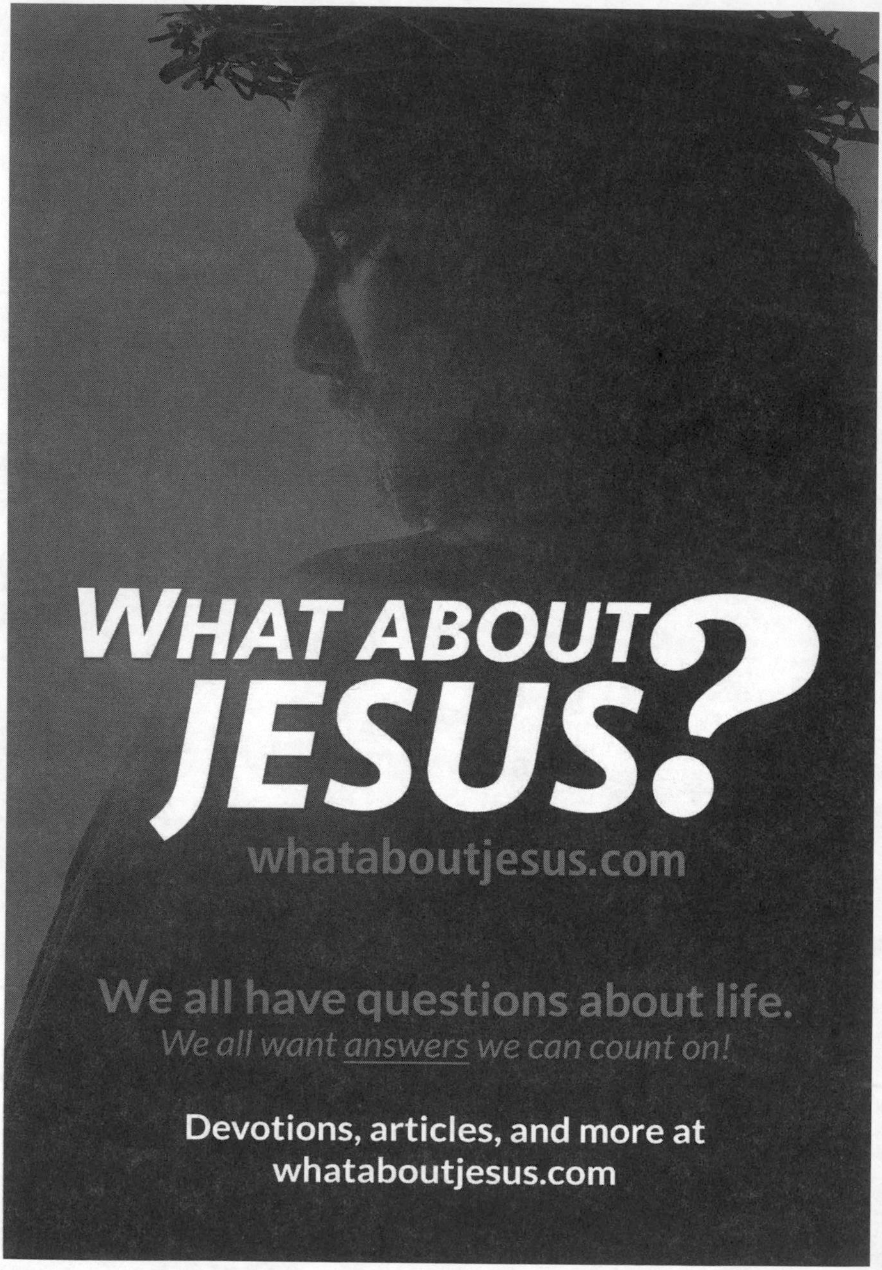
WHAT ABOUT JESUS?
whataboutjesus.com
We all have questions about life.
We all want answers we can count on!
Devotions, articles, and more at
whataboutjesus.com